Speaking of Critical Thinking

Peter Vincent
Naoko Nakazato

NAN'UN-DO

Download Audio

音声ファイル
無料 DL
のご案内

このテキストの音声を無料で視聴（ストリーミング）・ダウンロードできます。自習用音声としてご活用ください。
以下のサイトにアクセスしてテキスト番号で検索してください。

https://nanun-do.com　テキスト番号［**512080**］

※ 無線 LAN（WiFi）に接続してのご利用を推奨いたします。

※ 音声ダウンロードは Zip ファイルでの提供になります。
お使いの機器によっては別途ソフトウェア（アプリケーション）の導入が必要となります。

Read by

Rachel Walzer
Bianca Allen
Dominic Allen
Josh Keller

※ Speaking of Critical Thinking 音声ダウンロードページは以下の QR コードからもご利用になれます。

Speaking of Critical Thinking

Speaking of Critical Thinking

Preface

Welcome to **Speaking of Critical Thinking**, a textbook that provides you with an understanding of, and practice with, critical thinking. Critical thinking is not taught very much in Japan, but it is a very important life skill. While this textbook provides several short reading passages about the various steps and aspects of critical thinking, its main focus is on student experience with logic, creative thinking, and communication. It includes many case studies and communication activities based on the belief that one "Ah-hah!" experience is worth several "Uh-huh" moments. The text is designed for a student-centered class for active communication and is especially suited for pair work and small-group work.

To benefit most from this book, please remember: Don't be afraid of making mistakes. Making mistakes and learning from them is how you can improve your critical thinking as well as your English-communication skills.

I enjoyed writing this book and I hope that you will have an exciting time learning and speaking about critical thinking.

CONTENTS

Unit 1

Critical Thinking

クリティカル・シンキング（批判的思考）

1 Reading: Critical Thinking

リーディング：クリティカル・シンキング

The world is changing faster and faster, creating new sources of information and new challenges for everyone. For this reason, critical thinking is more important than ever before. We all need a systematic way* to examine new information, to come up with* various options to solve problems, and finally to use a logical approach to choose the best solutions.

Critical thinkers do not just accept information passively. They question the information and the sources and make independent decisions*. They try to see the whole picture* by considering different arguments and points of view. Moreover, they avoid jumping to conclusions* when making important or complex* decisions. Instead*, they try to understand a problem clearly, analyze it, and identify* various solutions before picking the best one.

This book provides a variety of case studies and activities to help you improve your critical thinking and problem-solving skills*. In addition, you will have practice in communicating your opinions about, and solutions to, different issues. Remember that critical thinking is not a natural talent. It is a skill to be developed. We can all improve our critical thinking and communication skills with practice!

* systematic way 系統的な方法　come up with 考え出す　independent decision 自主的な判断
whole picture 全体像　jump to conclusions 慌てて結論を出す　complex 複雑な
instead 代わりに　identify 確認する　problem-solving skills 問題解決スキル

The basic steps for critical thinking are:

1. Gathering important information about a problem or task.
2. Deciding what information is important and what is true (or not!).
3. Considering your strengths, weaknesses, values, and biases.*
4. Imagining the outcomes for various problem-solving choices.
5. Using logic to make the best plans and choices.
6. Imagining creative and sometimes unique solutions.
7. Explaining things clearly and presenting opinions well.
8. Learning from the results of your decisions, from both the successes and the failures.

*bias 偏見、先入観

True or False 内容把握

Write "T" if the sentence is true and "F" if the sentence is false.

以下の文章が内容と合っていれば "T"、合っていなければ "F" を空欄に書きましょう。

______ 1. Determining what information is true or not is an important life skill.

______ 2. It is important to consider various options before choosing one solution.

______ 3. It is important to make decisions about complex problems quickly.

______ 4. If you are not good at critical thinking now, you probably never will be.

______ 5. Being self-aware* is an important part of critical thinking.

______ 6. Imagination is a useful skill for critical thinking.

______ 7. Coming up with good solutions is not enough. You also need to communicate them clearly.

______ 8. Failure is never good or useful.

*self-aware 自覚している

2 Case Study: The Academic Advisor

ケーススタディ：アカデミックアドバイザー

A Japanese student named Risa came to her academic advisor at her university and said that she was very depressed.

"What's the problem?" the advisor asked.

"I don't like my classes. I'm tired and unmotivated*."

"Many students feel that way. Don't worry. You're going to graduate in just one more year, and then you can start your new life as an elementary-school teacher."

"But I don't want to be a teacher. I never wanted to be a teacher."

"Really? Then why did you choose to study Education?"

"Because my parents pushed me to become a teacher," the student answered. "They know I like children, and they told me it was a sure way to get a job."

The young woman had thought about changing her major* after her first year of study, but she was afraid it would have taken her another year to graduate. The delay* might have reduced her chances to get a job. Also, she believed her parents would have been unhappy about the extra expense and would have considered their daughter irresponsible*.

The advisor had to be careful about what she said to the student, for her department did not want to lose any students. Also, the university pushed graduates in the Education Department to become public-school teachers because it was good for the university's reputation*.

"Don't worry so much. You need to endure*. I'm sure you can do it," the advisor told the student.

After her talk with the advisor, the student was even more depressed and thought about dropping out* of school.

*unmotivated やる気のない　major 専攻　delay 遅れ　irresponsible 無責任な
reputation 評判　endure 我慢する　drop out 退学する

Questions to consider:

1. Why did this problem happen?
2. Is this a common or uncommon problem in Japan? Why?
3. What mistakes did the student make? What about her advisor and parents?
4. What do you think the student should do now?

3 Pair Work: Out of Place　ペアワーク：仲間外れ

Each of the word groups below has one word that does not belong. Find the word and circle it. Then write down why you think that word is out of place. The first one has been done for you.

1から10の単語群の中にひとつだけグループに属さないものがあります。その単語を○で囲み、属さない理由を書きましょう。

1. computer, printer, copy machine, (pen) *The other three items are office equipment.*
2. golf, swimming, soccer, tennis ______________________
3. beans, peaches, strawberries, bananas ______________________
4. arm, eyes, nose, ears ______________________
5. India, Japan, The United States, Africa ______________________
6. teacher, engineer, student, doctor ______________________
7. dog, lion, elephant, giraffe ______________________
8. run, walk, jump, jog ______________________
9. cello, piano, violin, guitar ______________________
10. leave, come, depart, go ______________________

4 Reading: Advertising　リーディング：広告

04

Advertising is a useful tool for understanding the steps of critical thinking. We can learn from how advertisers* communicate a message to people, often in a very creative and effective way. The people working in advertising companies go through* various steps of critical thinking in order to make their advertisements effective. They also have to work as a group, meaning communication and teamwork are important. Advertisers have a very clear goal: to get the target market* to buy their products or to get them to take an action*.

We can look at ads and consider them from different perspectives*, asking such questions as, "What is the product or message?" "Who is the advertisement trying to communicate to (in other words, who is the target market)?" "What is the connection between the headline and the visual?" and "What makes the advertisement effective or ineffective*?" Often, the headline and copy catch our interest*, sometimes with hidden or double meanings*. The language of advertisements is carefully chosen. It is often informal*, like the language used between friends, because this way of communicating makes us feel closer to the product or advertiser.

* advertiser 広告主　go through 経る　target market 目標とする市場
take an action 行動を起こす　perspective 見方　ineffective 効果のない
catch one's interest（人の）興味をつかむ　double meanings 二通りに取れる意味
informal 堅苦しくない、くだけた

Key Words

DRIVING WHILE TEXTING CAN BE A VERY GRAVE THING.

Headline

Visual

The grave* facts: driving while texting causes one out of every* four accidents in the U.S. It causes over nine deaths every day and almost 400,000 injuries every year. In fact, texting drivers are six times more likely* to cause an accident than drunk drivers.

Body copy

Drivers Against Texting — Sponsor

DAT@mgn.com — Contact information

* grave 深刻な、墓　　one out of every ~ 〜に1（人、回など）
~ times more likely ~ 〜倍も〜する可能性が高い

Questions to consider:

1. Why do you think headlines and visuals are usually large in advertisements?
2. What makes an effective advertisement?
3. What is the sponsor of this ad most concerned about?

5 Activity: Analyzing an Advertisement アクティビティ：広告を分析する

Look at the advertisement on page 11 and answer the following questions.
11ページの広告を見て、以下の質問に答えましょう。

1. The word "grave" in the headline has two different meanings. What are they?
   Meaning #1: ______________________________
   Meaning #2: ______________________________

2. What is the connection between the headline and the visual?
   What message do they send to the reader?
   ____

3. How does the body copy support the headline and the visual?
   ____

4. Is this an effective advertisement? Why or why not?
   ____

6 Group Discussion: Decision Making グループディスカッション：意思決定

Questions:

1. How do you make important decisions in your life? Do you have a usual approach or a system to make decisions?
2. Are you more logical or do you also use your intuition* when making decisions?
3. What types of decisions are you usually good at? What types of decisions are you not so good at? Why do you think you have these differences?
4. Are you creative? How do you show your creativity?
5. Are you good at communicating your ideas? Are you uncomfortable with speaking in front of groups?

*intuition 直観力

7 Reading: Brainstorming リーディング：ブレインストーミング

Brainstorming is a technique to help people come up with original ideas or solutions to tricky problems. It encourages* people to be open to any and all ideas, including ideas that may seem unusual at first. Brainstorming is often a group activity in which participants* are asked to avoid criticizing or even analyzing ideas at the initial* stage, for such judgments* can get in the way of* original thinking and limit creativity. Instead, brainstorming provides an open, supportive environment that encourages participation by all members. Evaluation* and selection of ideas are done at a later stage.

Brainstorming is not just an effective way to come up with original ideas and solutions. It can also spark fresh ideas and approaches at a later stage when ideas are more thoroughly* analyzed.

* encourage 奨励する　participant 参加者　initial 初期の　judgment 判断
get in the way of ~ ～の妨げになる　evaluation 評価　thoroughly 十分に

8 Activity: Setting Goals アクティビティ：ゴール設定

In the following activity, you are to brainstorm a list of goals you would like to achieve. The goals can be big or small, simple or difficult, realistic or idealistic, specific or vague. Do not judge your ideas, but instead let them pop up naturally into your mind. Write down at least eight in the spaces below.

以下のアクティビティでは、自分が達成したいゴールのリストを考えます。ゴールは大きくても小さくても、簡単でも難しくても、現実的でも非現実的でも、具体的でもあいまいでもかまいません。ゴールとして適切であるかどうかを考える必要はありません。自然に思いついたものを最低8個以上書き出してみましょう。

Examples: I want to lose weight. / I want to travel overseas. / I want to get better grades.

1. ______________________
2. ______________________
3. ______________________
4. ______________________
5. ______________________
6. ______________________
7. ______________________
8. ______________________
9. ______________________
10. ______________________

9 Pair Work: Riddles ペアワーク：なぞなぞ

1. Two mothers and two daughters sit together at a table in a restaurant. However, there are only three people at the table. How can this be?
2. A doctor was driving his car on a stormy night when he saw a car hit a tree on the road in front of him. He ran to the car and saw a young man in the driver's seat.
   "Oh, no!" the doctor said. "It's my son!"
   He drove his injured son to the hospital and helped him into the emergency room. "My son was in a car accident!" he told a nurse.
   The nurse put the man in a wheelchair and pushed him into another room. Another doctor came into the room and said "Oh, no! My son!"
   How is this possible?
3. What can you hold in your right hand but never in your left hand?

Unit 2
Logic and Organizing
論理と体系化

1 Activity: Life Challenge アクティビティ：人生の課題

Look at the pictures (A to M) below, which tell the story about the challenges of a student named Greg. Use the pictures to put the sentences in the correct order, numbering them from 1 to 13. The first one has been done for you.

A から M の絵は、Greg という学生が経験した人生の課題を表したものです。絵を参考にしながら、ストーリーの筋が通るよう空欄に文の順番（1~13）を入れましょう。

A

B

C

D

E

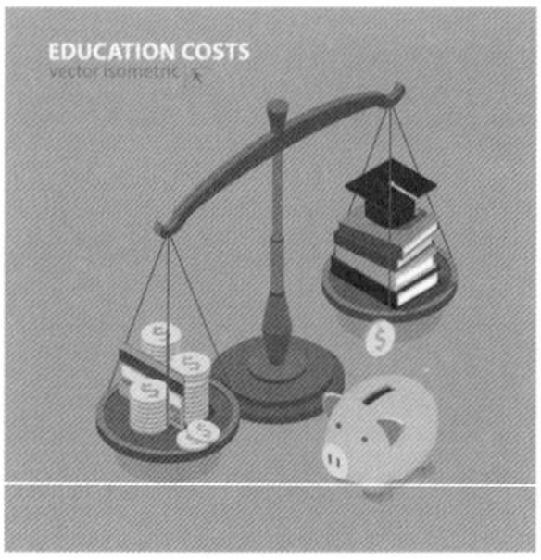

F

G

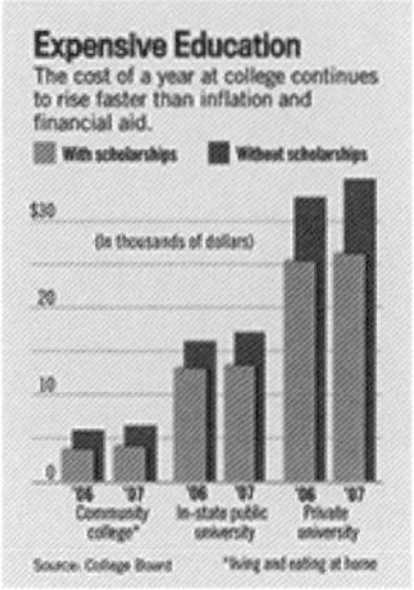

H

I

J

K　　L　　M

____ Greg graduated from high school. He was happy because he had saved thousands of dollars.

____ He understood their situation and thought about what to do, writing the ideas down on a list.

____ The counselor explained that costs at two-year community colleges were much cheaper than private universities, so he suggested that Greg attend the local community college first.

____ His father's medical costs were high, so his parents would not be able to help Greg with future university costs.

____ After two years at the community college, he transferred to the university of his dreams. The tuition* was expensive, but he had saved enough money.

____ He discovered the costs of attending the university were very high, so he knew he would have to save up a lot of money.

__1__ Greg had always planned to go to university since he was a kid.

____ Third, Greg looked for part-time job openings.* He wanted to start saving money.

____ First, he checked online to see what the tuition and living costs would be for the private university he hoped to attend.

____ He found a job as a dishwasher* in a local* restaurant and worked on weekends and during summers.

____ He continued to work at the restaurant while he studied at the community college, but as a waiter.

____ However, when he was in high school, his father had a bad car accident, which changed his plans.

____ Second, he made an appointment with a high-school counselor and asked his mother to join him.

*tuition 学費　job opening（仕事の）空き　dishwasher 洗い場担当　local 地元の

Questions:

1. What steps of critical thinking did Greg use?
2. Why was Greg successful?
3. Did these experiences somehow handicap Greg or did they make him stronger?

2 Activity: Organizing Words アクティビティ：順序を決める

Below are eight lists with four words each. Arrange the words in a way that is logical to you. Then write the type of system (i.e. alphabetical order, chronological order, etc.) you use for organizing words. Use different organization approaches when possible.

以下の８つのリストには、それぞれ４つの単語が書かれています。どのような理由で（例：アルファベット順、時系列など）順序を決めたのかを書いてみましょう。もしできれば異なる方法を使って順序を決めてみましょう。

Examples:

◇ adult, teenager, baby, child

Order : *baby, child, teenager, adult*

Ordered by : *Age (chronological order)*

◇ birdhouse, house, tent, castle

Order : *birdhouse, tent, house, castle*

Ordered by : *Size*

or

Order : *birdhouse, castle, house, tent*

Ordered by : *Alphabetical order*

1. sunset, afternoon, sunrise, night

Order : ______________________

Ordered by : ______________________

2. Japan, China, Canada, New Zealand

Order : ______________________

Ordered by : ______________________

3. William Prout, Judith Gomez, Gregory Stone, Stella Lin

Order : ______________________

Ordered by : ______________________

4. leaf, seed, branch, tree

Order : ______________________

Ordered by : ______________________

5. hour, day, minute, second

Order : ______________________

Ordered by : ______________________

6. neck, chest, stomach, head

Order : ______________________

Ordered by : ______________________

7. strawberries, grapes, watermelons, bananas

Order : ______________________

Ordered by : ______________________

8. university, high school, elementary school, middle school

Order : ______________________

Ordered by : ______________________

3 Activity: Finding a Connection アクテビティ：共通点を見つける

The following pairs of words may look like they are unrelated at first glance, but try to write two ways that they have something in common.

以下のワードペアの共通点を２つ探して書いてみましょう。

1. puppy/baby
   A: ______
   B: ______

2. computer/smartphone
   A: ______
   B: ______

3. newspaper/television
   A: ______
   B: ______

4. strawberry/tomato
   A: ______
   B: ______

5. water/wind
   A: ______
   B: ______

6. bubble/balloon
   A: ______
   B: ______

7. 5/9
   A: ______
   B: ______

8. lion/gorrila
   A: ______
   B: ______

9. earth/moon
   A: ______
   B: ______

10. fireman/doctor
   A: ______
   B: ______

4 Case Study: Logic ケーススタディ：論理性

06

A British man, Charles, read the editorial in the English-language version of a large Japanese newspaper. The English in the article was a little strange and too formal, but it was the style of writing that was a real mystery to Charles. The purpose of the article was unclear at first, and the writer wrote about several different issues, some seemingly unrelated to each other. However, the conclusion finally made the opinion of the writer and purpose of the article clear.

"Why did the writer wait until the end to make his point clear?" Charles wondered. "What a frustrating article!"

Questions:

1. Why do you think the article was written in this style?
2. Why was Charles so frustrated?

5 Activity: Find the Statement アクティビティ：主張を見つける

Find the statement in each of the following lists of sentences and write "S" in the blank. Then find three support sentences and write "SS" in the blanks. Finally, find the sentence in each list that has no relationship to the others and write "X" in the blank.

以下のリストの中で、主張文には "S" を、裏付け文には "SS" を、他と全く関係のない文には "X" を空欄に書き入れましょう。

A. ____ Our stress becomes reduced.
____ Research shows that exercise is good for us.
____ Our physical health improves.
____ Vegetables are good for our health.
____ We have more strength and energy.

B. ____ Rich people are usually happier than poor people.
____ Taking trips and sharing experiences with others make us happy.
____ The way that we spend money affects our happiness.
____ Research shows that giving to others increases our life satisfaction.
____ Buying expensive things does not make us happier in the long run.

C. ____ They feel less lonely by having a cat, dog, or other pet.
____ Caring for a pet is fun and gives more meaning to their lives.
____ Research shows that elderly people with pets are often healthier and live longer.
____ Dogs have better personalities than cats.
____ Having a pet can improve the lives of elderly people who live alone.

6 Activity: Support Sentences アクティビティ：裏付け文

Choose one of the statements below (check the box) and then write four supporting sentences for that statement.

以下の主張文の中から1つ選び、その意見に対する裏付け文を4つ作りましょう。

- ☐ Japan needs to allow more foreign workers into Japan.
- ☐ The government should tax plastic garbage.
- ☐ Tabaco should be banned in all public places.
- ☐ Parents should not give smartphones to children under 10 years old.
- ☐ Parents should not send their children to cram schools.

1. ______________________________
2. ______________________________
3. ______________________________
4. ______________________________

7 Activity: Setting a Goal アクティビティ：ゴール設定

Look back at the list of goals you brainstormed in Activity 8 of Unit 1 on page 13. Choose one of these goals: a larger goal that is important to you would be the best. You may come up with a new goal if you would prefer. Make sure your goal is specific and clear. This makes your goal easier to achieve. It also helps you create a plan to reach your goal, which we will do in a later activity.

Unit 1のActivity 8 (p.13) でゴール設定についてブレインストーミングしたことを思い出し、そのゴールの中から1つを選んでください。できれば自分にとって最も重要な、大きめのゴールを選びましょう。新しいゴールを作っても構いません。自分のゴールが具体的で明確であることを確認しましょう。明確であるほどゴールを達成しやすくなるからです。また後で行う、ゴール達成の計画を作るアクティビティがやりやすくなります。

Vague Goal	Clear goal
I want to lose weight.	I want to lose six kilos.
I want to save money.	I want to save ¥100,000 by the end of this year.
I want to become good at English.	I want to pass Eiken Grade Pre-1 by next year.

Write the goal in the box below, and write why this goal is important to you. Be prepared to share your goal and its importance to you.

下の枠内にゴールとなぜこのゴールが自分にとって大事なのかを書き入れ、それらをシェアできるようにしてください。

8 Pair Work : Logic Games ペアワーク：論理性ゲーム

Try to solve the three problems below.
以下の３つの問題を解いてください。

A. Take away three matchsticks to make three triangles.

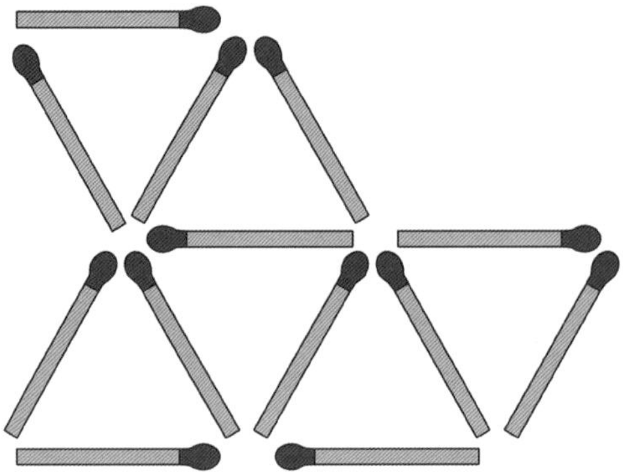

B. Move one matchstick in each equation to make them correct.

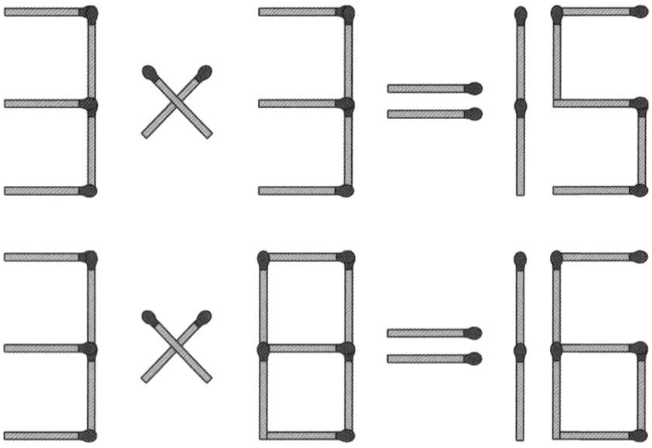

C. Take away three matchsticks in each equation to make them correct.

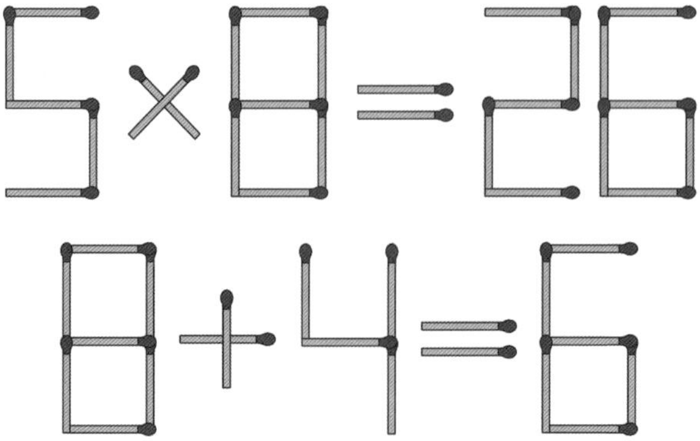

Unit 3
Strategies
ストラテジー

1 Activity: Connecting the Dots

アクティビティ：点と点を結びつける

"Connecting the dots" is an English expression that means to try to make sense of information that is incomplete. We often do this during our daily lives. Can you tell what the picture to the right is by mentally "connecting the dots"?

"Connecting the dots" とは、不完全な情報を繋げて意味を見出す、という意味です。これは私たちが日常行っていることです。点と点を繋がずに右の絵が何か想像できますか？

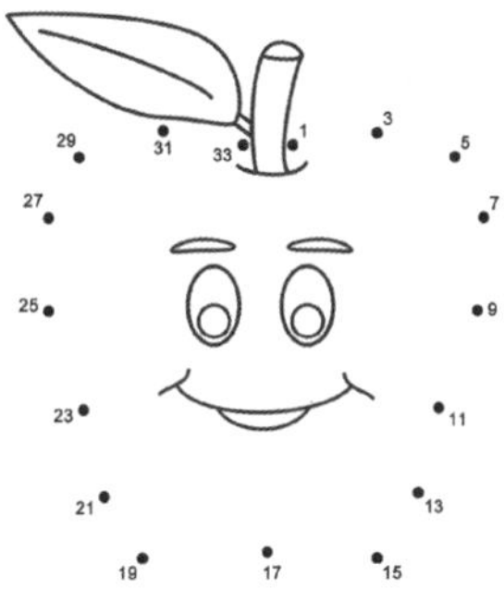

To the left is a famous puzzle that requires you to connect the dots. There are nine dots. Connect them with four straight lines. However, you cannot lift your pen or pencil when drawing the four lines.

左の絵は点と点を結びつけないとわからないパズルです。ペンを紙から離さずに、9つの点を4本の線で結んでください。

When we face a new problem, we sometimes must "think outside the box," which is to look at things in a fresh way and come up with a good solution. We have to use our imagination and be flexible. Thinking outside the box helps us think creatively and become better critical thinkers.

2 Activity: Advertising Analysis アクティビティ：広告の分析

Look at the product advertisements in Appendix 1A, 1B, 1C, and 1D on pages 97 to 99 and answer the following questions.

Appendix 1A、1B、1C、1D（p.97～p.99）の広告を見て、以下の質問に答えましょう。

Appendix 1A

1. What is the product? ____________________
2. Why did the headline focus on French fries? ____________________
____
3. What is the target audience for this product? ____________________
4. What is the benefit that the ad mentions? ____________________
5. What makes the sentence in the body copy catchy?* ____________________
6. What kind of media would be effective for this ad? ____________________

*catchy　人の心を捉える

Appendix 1B

1. What is the product? ____________________
2. How do the headline and picture work together? ____________________
3. What is the target audience for this product? ____________________
4. What are the benefits the ad mentions or hints at? ____________________
____
5. What kind of media would be effective for this ad? ____________________

Appendix 1C

1. What is the product? ____________________
2. How do the headline and picture work together? ____________________
3. What is the main target audience for this product? ____________________
   What is a secondary target of the ad? ____________________
4. What are the benefits the ad mentions or hints at? ____________________
____
5. What kind of media would be effective for this ad? ____________________

Appendix 1D

1. What is the product? ____________________
2. What makes the headline catchy? ____________________
3. What is the target audience for this ad? ____________________
4. What kind of media would be effective for this ad? ____________________

3 Activity: Who Am I? アクティビティ：私は誰？

You will have the name of a famous person put on your back. Ask "yes/no" questions to get information to find out who you are. Ask one question to one person and then move to another person. When you find out who you are, tell the teacher.

グループ内の1人が自分の背中に有名人の名前を書いた紙を貼られます。紙を貼られた人は、グループ内の他のメンバーに、"Yes/No" で答えられる質問をして、自分が誰かを当ててください。当てたら先生に伝えましょう。

Example questions:

A: Am I a famous singer?
B: No, you're not.

A: Am I an actor?
C: Yes, you are.

A: Am I a man?
D: No, you're not.

A: Am I Japanese?
E: No.

Before you begin, prepare some questions to ask. Work with a group to make good questions in the chart below. What type of questions are good to begin with?

以下の表にいくつか質問があります。グループ内で話し合いながら、新しい質問を作り、表に加えてください。どんなことから聞いていったらよいでしょう？

Am I ...	Do I ...
a man? / a woman?	have black hair? wear glasses? appear on TV?

*appear on TV　TVに出演する

4 Group Work: Memory Challenge

グループワーク：記憶力チャレンジ

Work in groups. Each person in the group will look at the picture story in Appendix 2 on pages 100 and 101 for two minutes, trying to imagine and to remember the story. After closing the pages for Appendix 2, number the sentences below in the correct order, putting the verbs in the past tense. The 11th sentence has already been done for you. You may want to discuss how to approach this task (strategy) with your group before starting.

Appendix 2（p.100、p.101）の絵を2分間見たあと、絵を閉じてグループのメンバーと一緒にストーリーを想像してみましょう。ストーリーの筋が通るよう左側の空欄に番号を入れ、文中の空欄には動詞の過去形を入れてください。11番目にくる文にはすでに動詞を入れてあります。アクティビティをはじめる前にどう取りくむかをあらかじめメンバーと話し合いましょう。

____ He ____________ (run) outside to look, and one UFO ____________ (fly) over him.

____ Inside the UFO, he ____________ (see) two green aliens ____________ (come) towards him.

____ After many days, the UFO ____________________ (head back) to Earth.

____ Zac ____________ (wake) up at night. There ____________ (is) a strange light in his room.

____ He ____________ (see) three UFOs in the sky.

____ He ____________ (wave) goodbye, and the UFO ________________ (fly away).

____ They ____________ (take) him to another world. He ____________ (see) many new and strange things there.

____ Suddenly, he was ____________ (fly) in the sky toward the UFO.

____ The aliens ____________ (bring) him back to Earth. He ____________ ____________ (land on) the ground near his house.

____ He ____________ (enter) the UFO and ____________ (find) himself in a large, strange room.

__11__ They __landed on__ (land on) another planet and then they __let__ (let) him walk. He __walked into__ (walk into) a strange-looking forest.

____ He ____________ (go) to his bedroom window and ____________ (look) outside.

____ The aliens ____________ (come close) and ____________ (speak) to him.

____ He ____________________ (look out) the window of the UFO and ____________ (see) the Earth far below.

5 Group Activity: Pictionary

グループアクティビティ：ピクショナリー

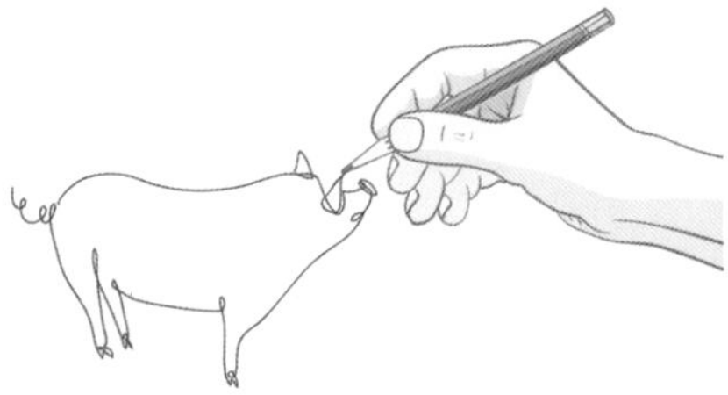

You will play a game. In a team, one person will draw a picture (the artist), and the other team members should try to guess the word in English. Artists who hear the correct word should raise their hand to win a point. The teacher will explain how to play in more detail.

ゲームをしましょう。チームの中で最初に絵を描く人を決めます。ほかのチームメンバーはその絵が何かを英語であててください。絵を描いている人は、メンバーが正しい答えを言ったら、すぐに手を挙げてください。一番最初に正しい答えをあてたチームにポイントが入ります。詳細については先生が詳しく説明します。

6 Group Activity: Survival Game

グループアクティビティ：サバイバルゲーム

Imagine you are in a small airplane that crashes into the sea near a small tropical island. You only have time to get 8 items from the plane. You will likely spend several weeks or even months on the island with five other survivors. The island has a small river and many coconut trees.

自分の乗っている飛行機が、熱帯の小さな無人島の近くに墜落したと想定してみましょう。飛行機からは８つのアイテムを持ち出すことができます。生き残った残りの５人と数週間、あるいは数か月過ごさなければなりません。島には小さな川とたくさんのヤシの木があります。

The items you can choose from:

８つのアイテムは以下のリストから選べます。

☐ 10 bottles of drinking water
☐ A can opener*
☐ A copy of a book called "Surviving in the Wilderness"*
☐ A book called "Edible* Wild Plants in the Tropics"*
☐ A box with 5 blankets
☐ A kit with two hunting knives and a small axe*
☐ Soap
☐ 6 changes of clothes
☐ A flashlight* with batteries*
☐ Rope
☐ 30 pounds of hamburger meat
☐ A device that converts* saltwater into drinking water
☐ 6 raincoats
☐ A complete fishing kit
☐ A box with 20 cans of vegetables
☐ A large box of matches
☐ 5 bathing suits
☐ Large boxes of salt and pepper
☐ 2 large bags of potatoes
☐ A large tent
☐ A compass
☐ A small rubber* raft*
☐ A metal helmet

*can opener 缶切り　wilderness 荒野、原野　edible 食用の　tropics 熱帯地域　axe 斧
flashlight 懐中電灯　battery 電池　convert 変換する　rubber ゴム製の　raft いかだ

7 Writing: Reaching Your Personal Goal

ライティング：自分のゴールを達成するためのストラテジー

Look back at the goal you selected in Activity 7 of Unit 2 on page 19. Write down the goal again and then write down smaller steps, each with a clear goal and dates that will lead to the completion of your goal. It is not too late to come up with a better or more important goal if you want!

Activity 7の Unit 2 (p.19) で選んだゴールを見てみましょう。ゴールをもう一度書き出したら、それぞれのゴールについて明確なスモールステップとゴール達成の日付も書きましょう。前回より大事なゴールができたら、変えることも可能です！

Example:

Goal: ***Get a job at a major trading company.***

Steps To Achieve My Goal	Date
1. *Finish a powerful resume. Have it checked by my university's employment center.*	*June*
2. *Go to a job fair to learn about eight or more companies.*	*Before the end of August*
3. *Do in-depth research on five target companies.*	*By the end of summer*
4. *Send out applications to at least three companies.*	*November*
5. *Receive invitations to interviews at companies.*	*January*
6. *Get at least one job offer!*	*February*

Goal: ____

Steps To Achieve My Goal	Date
1.	
2.	
3.	
4.	
5.	
6.	

8 Group Activity: Japan's Empty Houses

グループアクティビティ：日本の空き家

Japan has about 8.5 million vacant homes, called *akiya*. Many villages and towns across Japan are no longer livable because of the loss of workers, taxes, and support systems, such as hospitals, schools, and public transportation. By 2040, 7.2 million hectares, an area about the size of Ireland, will become unclaimed land.

日本には約 850 万件の空き家があるといわれています。日本の村や町の多くが人手、税金、病院、学校、公共交通機関などの支援システムの不足で人が住めない状況です。2040 年までにアイルランドの面積に相当する、720 万ヘクタールの土地が引き取り手のない土地となるとされています。

Options: Work in a group and discuss strategies for one of the following:

1. Ways to help one or more dying villages
2. How empty houses could become a new business opportunity
3. Ways the government could make use of unclaimed land

9 Pair Work : Investment Strategy

ペアワーク：投資のストラテジー

Imagine you have about 100 million yen of your own to invest. Your aim is to make a profit. Where would you invest? Use the internet to do some research and prepare a presentation explaining your strategy. Do you choose a safe approach or go for higher risk and higher profit? Do you have other goals, such as helping people or improving the environment? Why?

今自分には投資できるお金が1億円あると仮定してください。自分の目的は利益を生むことです。何に投資しますか？　インターネットを使ってリサーチをし、自分のストラテジーを説明するプレゼンテーションを準備してください。安全な手段を選びますか？　それとも高利益、高リスクの手段を選びますか？　それはなぜですか？

Presentation Organization: You should start your presentation with a statement, and then give supporting arguments.

Example: Hello, everyone, We'd like to invest in an apartment building and make it a sharehouse for foreigners and Japanese. There are three reasons we decided on a sharehouse. First, We want to ...

Unit 4
Culture
文化

1 Case Study: Tea and Cake
ケーススタディ：お茶とケーキ

An American man works at a private Japanese university. He is a professor in the British and American Cultures Department. He enjoys working at the school, even though it is very traditional. He noticed during the monthly department meetings that the two female Japanese professors were the ones to always serve cake, tea, or other snacks to the other professors, all male. The American thought this was odd, especially in a department called "British and American Cultures," so he decided to get up and help the women. He thought that by setting an example, the Japanese male professors might change their ways and help serve. However, nothing changed. For several years, he was the only male to help the two women.

Questions:

1. Why did this happen?
2. Is gender equality* in Japan changing? Do you think it will change in the future?

*gender equality 男女平等

2 Case Study: The Homework Assignment
ケーススタディ：宿題

An American man is married to a Japanese woman, and they live in Japan. Their young son, Tristan, went to a neighborhood elementary school. The man plans to move back to the U.S. in the future, so the couple decided to send Tristan to an international school in Tokyo when he finished the third grade. At the new school, the boy did not speak English as well as other students, so he struggled to catch up.

One day, the father came home from work and saw that his wife was upset. "Tristan's having trouble doing his homework. I tried to help him, but I didn't succeed. Now, it's your turn."

The man went to his son's room and saw him crying in front of his computer.

"What's wrong?" asked the father.

"I don't know what to write!" said Tristan.

"What's the assignment?" asked the father.

"I have to write a story about the future and about space."

"That sounds like fun!" said the father. "We can choose a planet in space, add people, aliens, robots, whatever we want."

Tristan cried more loudly. "But it may be the wrong answer. The teacher didn't tell us which planet or what things to say."

"But that's up to you*. We can make any story we want. There's no right answer in story-making."

"You don't understand! I don't want to make a mistake!"

The father thought back to the class observation* he did at his son's Japanese school. He was impressed with how well organized it was and how well behaved the children were. Did Tristan's current problem have something to do with the change from a Japanese educational approach to a Western approach?

*up to ~ ～しだい　class observation 授業参観

Questions:

1. Why did Tristan have such a big problem with his homework assignment?
2. What does his problem say about the Japanese system of education?

3 Case Study: Money and Marital Problems

ケーススタディ：お金と結婚の問題

09

A British man named Ronald fell in love with a Japanese woman named Reiko, and after dating for a few years, they decided to marry. Ron thought Reiko was perfect for him, but he did have one worry. She worked full-time, and even though she lived with her parents and ate her mother's food, she spent all the money she earned and had nothing left by the end of each month. Ron had worked since the age of 14 and had always saved part of his earnings, for he planned to go to college. Years later, he paid for most of his university education. He was also frugal* by nature*.

After they married, Ron and Reiko had a baby, and Reiko quit her job to take care of the baby. Reiko's parents helped take care of the baby, too, so Ron was surprised that Reiko did not want to get a job for several years, even a part-time job. The couple were soon short of money.

After quitting her job, Reiko told Ron that she wanted to receive his monthly paycheck and manage their money. Ron thought that it was unfair: he earned all of the family income*, but Reiko controlled the money. Moreover, she gave him only a small allowance. The couple fought over money and how much allowance Ron should get.

Several years later, Reiko finally got a part-time job. However, she still wanted her husband's paycheck*. It became clear to Ron, however, that she felt his salary was the family's money, while her income was hers to spend as she wanted. She took several overseas trips with her friends, trips that Ron could not afford. He became very frustrated with their financial arrangement and wondered if he had made a bad choice in marriage.

* frugal 倹約家の　by nature もともと（生まれつき）　income 収入　paycheck 給料

Questions:

1. Is Ronald right to feel frustrated with the couple's financial arrangement?
2. Why do you think Reiko acts the way she does?

4 Case Study: The Critical Husband

ケーススタディ：批判的な夫

An American was invited to the house of a middle-aged Japanese government official. The official introduced his wife, and then the two men sat at a table for dinner while the wife served drinks and food. The wife had prepared a beautiful dinner, and the American was enjoying the food.

The wife brought in another dish, some very delicious-looking *tempura*.

"I'm sorry that my wife's such a poor cook. I hope you can eat it," said the husband. "I also wish she were prettier."

The wife smiled and didn't look hurt by the comment. However, the American was shocked. The wife was doing everything for her husband, yet he seemed to show no appreciation. "Their relationship must be bad. Maybe they'll divorce* in the future," thought the American.

*divorce 離婚（する）

Questions:

1. Why did the Japanese husband act this way?
2. Why do you think the American was shocked?

5 Case Study: The Chopsticks ケーススタディ：お箸 11

An American was invited to a Japanese home for dinner. During the meal, the American stuck his chopsticks in his bowl of rice so that they stood up in the rice. His Japanese host looked shocked, so the American realized he had done something wrong.

Questions:

1. What mistake did the American make?
2. Why is it a mistake to do this in Japan?

6 Case Study: The Ski Trip ケーススタディ：スキー旅行 12

An American joined a group of Japanese workers from his company for a two-day ski trip. In the morning, the American and other experienced skiers taught and helped the beginner skiers. After lunch at a restaurant on the ski slope, the group decided to go back to the hotel to play some games and do other activities together.

The American told everyone that he would ski by himself, since (like everyone) he had bought a day pass. He felt he had already done his group activity in the morning and wanted some free time to do some more challenging skiing. When he returned to the hotel late in the afternoon, his other colleagues* were cool to him.

* colleague 同僚

Questions:

1. Why do you think the Japanese colleagues were cool to the American?
2. What does this say about Japanese culture?

7 Activity: Global Village アクティビティ：グローバルヴィレッジ

The world population is over 7.5 billion people (7,500,000,000). If you think of the world as a global village with just 100 people, the variety of people is easier to imagine. Look at the information below. With a partner, put the correct numbers in the spaces.

世界には 75 億人が住んでいます。地球上の人口がもし 100 人しかいなかったと仮定してみてください。世界の人々について色々なことが容易に想像できます。以下の情報を参考に、パートナーと相談し、最も適切と思われる数字を空欄に入れましょう。

75 50 50 25

In the village, there are ...

_____ females.

_____ males.

_____ children.

_____ adults.

14 60 10 16

In the village, there are ...

_____ Asians.

_____ Africans.

_____ people from the Americas.

_____ Europeans.

15 7 31 8 23 16

In the village, there are ...

_____ Christians.

_____ Muslims.

15 Hindus.

_____ Buddhists.

_____ people with no religion.

_____ people who believe in other religions.

12 6 5 2 2 73

In the village, there are ...

_____ people who speak English.

_____ people who speak Chinese.

_____ people who speak Spanish.

_____ people who speak Russian.

_____ people who speak Japanese.

73 people who speak other languages.

Source: https://www.100people.org/statistics_100stats.php?section=statistics

8 Group Discussion: English Proficiency in Japan

グループディスカッション：日本人の英語運用能力

Japanese students now study English over six years in school before university, though few students learn to speak English well. In one study on non-English speaking countries, Japan ranked 35th out of 72 countries for English proficiency.

Questions:

1. Do you think it is important that all students learn to speak English well? If not all students, which students should learn English?

2. The Japanese government has long aimed to increase English proficiency in Japan. Why have their efforts largely failed?

9 Simulation: Task Force to Improve English Proficiency

シミュレーション：英語運用能力を伸ばすための特別委員会

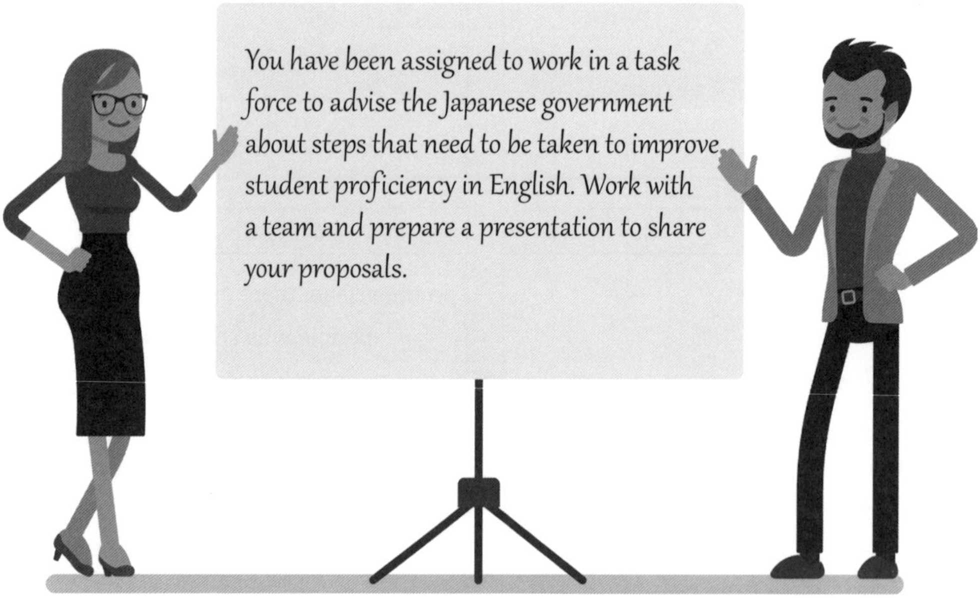

Unit 5
Communication
コミュニケーション

1 Case Study: A Communication Problem

ケーススタディ：コミュニケーションの問題

A Japanese student recently arrived in the U.S. and met with a foreign student counselor to talk about things he needed to do at the university. The counselor gave a lot of information to the student, who smiled and nodded*, but made no sound.

After several minutes, the counselor asked him, "Do you understand what I've been saying?"

"Yes, yes," the student answered, "It's a nice day."

The counselor realized the student hadn't understood most of her words, and she was frustrated because she had to start over.

*nod うなづく

Questions:

1. Why do you think the Japanese student acted this way?
2. What do you think he should have done in this situation?

2 Case Study: The Embarrassed Foreigner

14

ケーススタディ：困惑した外国人

A foreigner was walking in Tokyo Station behind a young woman. A young Japanese man accidentally hit the woman with his elbow when putting earplugs into his ear. Realizing what he had done, he quickly jumped out of the way.

The woman turned around and looked at the foreigner, thinking it was he who had hit her. The foreigner was shocked and did not know what to do or say (he spoke only a few words of Japanese), so he said "Sumimasen."

The Japanese woman became angry at him, but she finally turned around and walked away.

Questions:

What could the foreigner have done to communicate more effectively to the woman?

3 Case Study: The Postcard

ケーススタディ：絵ハガキ

15

A young Japanese woman who spoke very little English bought five postcards in a shop in the U.S. She found another postcard she liked and wanted to exchange it for one of the postcards she had already bought. She went back to the clerk, but there was no way she could say, "Excuse me. I'd like to exchange this postcard for one of the five that I've already bought. Would that be alright?" Still, she was able to communicate successfully.

Questions:

1. What do you think she said and did?
2. What does this say about "real communication"?

4 Activity: The Man from Another Time

アクティビティ：異時代の人

A man frozen in ice is discovered, and scientists bring him back to life. He speaks English, but he hasn't been conscious since 1702. Explain to him about some of the following things:

- Computers
- Automobiles
- Rock concerts
- Modern education
- Smartphones
- Airplanes
- Democracy
- Problems in today's world

5 Activity: Presenting Your Opinion アクティビティ：意見を述べる

In English-speaking countries, it is usually good to be direct and clear when presenting an opinion. The following steps generally apply:

1 **When arguing a point, we first say what we believe.**
"I think companies should pay a special tax to clean up pollution."

2 **You may want to give more details about, or clarification* of, your argument.**
"The companies that pollute more should pay a higher tax."

3 **Then you should give reasons why you have this opinion.**
"Companies should pay this tax because they will then want to reduce their pollution. Also, the government can use the money they collect from companies to help clean up polluted areas and keep our environment safe and clean."

*clarification 明確化

Look at the list of statements below. Pick one of the topics and prepare a short presentation. You will be asked to give your presentation to the class or a group of students.

以下の意見のリストから、ひとつトピックを選んで短いプレゼンテーションを準備し、クラスメイトの前で発表しましょう。

1. Smartphones should/should not be given to children.
2. People should pay tax for the plastic waste they throw away.
3. The internet should/should not be censored.*
4. Same-sex schools are good/bad for students.
5. High school students should/should not wear uniforms.
6. Animals should/should not be kept in zoos.
7. Parents should/should not send their children to cram schools.*
8. Smoking should/should not be banned in all restaurants and coffee shops.
9. Husbands should/should not share housework with their wives (Option: Children should/should not do house chores*).
10. Company management and political leaders should/should not be about 50% female.

* censor 検閲する　　cram school 塾　　chores 家事

Try to

1. Remember much of your speech so that you speak smoothly and have eye contact.

2. Speak slowly, clearly, and make sure you speak loudly enough.

3. Practice your pronunciation. Use simple words when possible. Avoid *katakana* English.

6 Activity: Text Messaging (1)

アクティビティ：携帯でメッセージ（1）

Text messages often have their own form of spelling and grammar.

携帯を使ったメールでは、特別な省略形やスペルを使うことがあります。

Example:

'*u*' which means 'you'
'*cu*' which means 'see you'
'*oc*' which means 'of course'

Match the text message on the left with the standard English on the right.

1～15の意味を、A～Oまでのメッセージから選びましょう。

____	1. *b4*	A.	to you
____	2. *ily*	B.	Are you OK?
____	3. *2u*	C.	before
____	4. *thx*	D.	Got to go.
____	5. *bc*	E.	Sorry.
____	6. *ur*	F.	by the way
____	7. *tho*	G.	because
____	8. *ttyl*	H.	Thanks.
____	9. *bff*	I.	Great!
____	10. *gtg*	J.	I love you.
____	11. *ruok*	K.	Talk to you later.
____	12. *ik*	L.	your
____	13. *btw*	M.	though
____	14. *sry*	N.	best friends forever
____	15. *gr8*	O.	I know.

7 Activity: Text Messaging (2)

アクティビティ：携帯でメッセージ (2)

Change the following text messages into standard English.

次のメッセージを普通の英文に直しましょう

Example: *c u later* See you later. *where ru?* Where are you?

1. *how ru?* ______________________ 2. *its 4u* ______________________

3. *i want 2go* ______________________ 4. *cu 2morrow* ______________________

5. *ur gr8!* ______________________________________

6. *do u want 2c a movie 2morrow?* ______________________________________

8 Group Discussion: Communication

グループディスカッション：コミュニケーション

Questions:

1. Are you good at communicating your ideas? At what times do you think you are at your communication best?
2. Are you uncomfortable with speaking in front of large groups?
3. Is communicating at times of conflict difficult for you? Do you think your communication is effective when you are feeling emotional? Why or why not?

9 Activity: Crossword Puzzle

アクティビティ：クロスワード

Communication in a foreign language can be a challenge. When we have limited vocabulary and grammar, we have to use different communication strategies to make ourselves clear. This is a kind of critical thinking.

Work in pairs. **Student A**: Look at page 41. **Student B:** Turn to Appendix 3 on page 102. Give hints to help your partner guess the words that you can see in your half of the crossword. But do not say the actual words in your hints. Then listen to your partner and write in the words that he/she is describing.

ペアになって、Student A はこのページを、Student B は Appendix 3 (p.102)を見てください。各自のクロスワードのすでに埋まっている単語をパートナーにあててもらいます。ヒントを出し合い、お互いのクロスワードの空欄を埋めましょう。答えを言ってしまわないように気を付けてください。

Example:

B: What's 8 down?

A: This is a verb. It's something you do when you want to make things neat.

B: Clean?

A: No. Let's say* you have a lot of books and you want to put them together by the type of book, such as textbooks, novels, comic books, and picture books. It's the opposite of "make a mess."

B: Organize!

A: Yes, that's it!

* Let's say ~ たとえば~したとして

Student A

1 p	e	1 t			2			3 d			4 m				
								o			e				5
6 s	e	a	r	c	h			7 g	8 o		8 a		9 p		
t							10 f		r		n		o		
r							u		g			11 g	o	a	l
a				12 p	l	a	n		13 a				r		
14 t									n						14 u
e			15 c	o	m	15 m	u	n	i	c	a	t	i	o	n
g		16 l							z						i
y		o				16 s	a	m	e						q
		17 s	18							19					u
20 d	r	e	a	m				20							e
						21 k	n	o	w	l	e	d	21 g	e	
22 t	22 h	i	n	k									a		
							23 u						23 m		
	24 t	h	a	n	k		25 p						e		

10 Pair Work: Role Plays ペアワーク：ロールプレイ

Your teacher will give you and your partner a communication problem. How can you communicate successfully? Prepare to act out your solution to the problem in front of the class.

先生がコミュニケーションに関する問題を提示します。どうしたらスムーズなコミュニケーションがとれるでしょうか？ 問題の解決策を実際にクラスの前で表現してみましょう。

Unit 6
Perception
感じ方

1 Activity: Illusions　アクティビティ：錯覚

Look at the three illustrations above. What do you see?　上の絵を見てください。何に見えますか？

Which line below is longer?　どちらが長いですか？

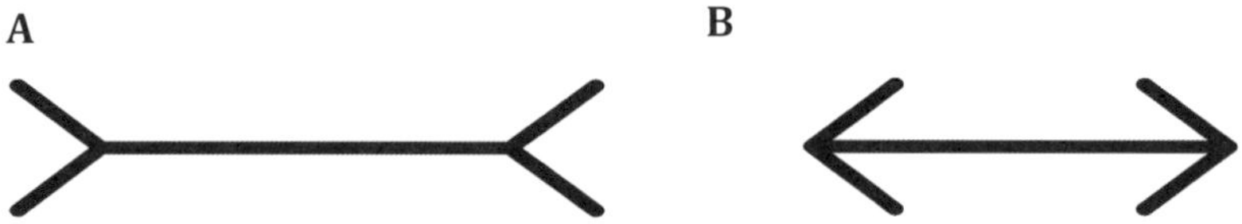

2 Reading: Perception　リーディング：感じ方

16

We often assume* that people see things the same way, since we all have human eyes. But people often see the same things differently (perception) and understand what they see (interpretation) in a different way. Consider how fans of baseball, soccer, fashion, or *kabuki* see and understand important details that others would miss. Culture also has a large effect on how individuals see things and interpret* their meaning.

Our perceptions of the world around us rely on* our five basic senses of sight, hearing, smell, taste, and touch. These are the main senses we use to experience the world. We constantly* get information from our senses, so much that we ignore* much of it. We usually perceive* those things that are important to us and ignore the rest*. These choices are also part of our own worldview and our own bias*. They are mostly unconscious*. It is important to recognize* that our perception can limit us in certain environments, especially if we are in different cultures, where we easily make mistakes. During communication with someone from a different culture, we may miss small but important cues*, from body language to changes in voice tone, from raised voices to silence.

Communication is much more than words. Nonverbal communication*, including hand gestures, facial expressions, eye contact, and body movement, is done for a variety of purposes. Some are made purposefully*, such as a gesture used to support an idea or a word. For example, a shrug of the shoulders and hands extended* upwards* in the U.S. supports the verbal expression, "I don't know." Sometimes, nonverbal communication can substitute* for a verbal message, for example, pointing to a watch to show "We have to go!" or "It's late," or holding up a thumb* to express "Great!" Nonverbal communication can also help regulate* verbal communication, such as a grunt* given to show that one is listening to another's communication (and have them continue speaking) or a "stop" hand gesture to halt* conversation.

When in a new environment or a foreign culture, our assumptions* of what words, gestures, and other things mean and our lack of awareness* of other cultural differences can cause serious problems.

*assume 思い込む、仮定する　interpret 解釈する　rely on ~ ～に頼る　constantly 常に
ignore 無視する　perceive ~ ～だと認識する　rest 残り　bias 偏見
unconscious 無意識の　recognize 認識する　cue 合図
nonverbal communication 非言語コミュニケーション　purposefully 意図的に　extend 伸ばす
upward 上に向かって　substitute 代わりのもの　thumb 親指　regulate 調節する
grunt 低いうなり声　halt 停止させる　assumption 思い込み、前提
awareness 自覚

True or False 内容把握

Write "T" if the sentence is true and "F" if the sentence is false.

内容と一致している場合は "T" を、一致していなければ "F" を入れましょう。

_____ 1. Differences in perception and interpretation* are all due to* cultural differences.

_____ 2. We usually perceive things that are not important to us.

_____ 3. We usually consciously choose what we want to see and what we want to ignore.

_____ 4. Facial expressions, such as a smile, have the same meanings in almost all cultures.

_____ 5. Nonverbal communication is used to support verbal messages, or it can be a message by itself.

*interpretation 解釈　due to ~ ～が原因で

3 Activity: Perception of Color

アクティビティ：色の認識

What do you think the following pictures show in terms of color and perception?

以下の絵は、色や知覚についてどんなことを表しているでしょう？

1

2

4 Activity: Different Interpretations

アクティビティ：異なる解釈

Look at the picture below. What the two women in the picture see is different, but their interpretation about "male dominated culture" is the same. Why is that? What does it say about their cultures?

以下の絵を見てください。2人の女性が見ているものは異なります。でも「男性社会の文化」に対する彼女たちの感じ方は同じです。それはなぜでしょう？　彼女たちの文化に関してどんなことが言えると思いますか？

5 Activity: Nonverval Communication

アクティビティ：非言語コミュニケーション

Match the communication expressed in the pictures with the sentences below.

以下の絵は何を伝えようとしているのでしょうか？　1～16の英語表現を表す絵をA～Pの中から選んでください。

A

B

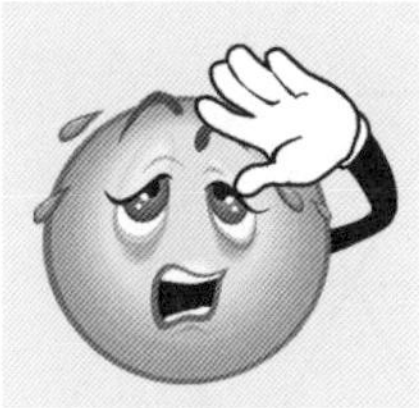

C

D

E

F

G

H

I

J

K

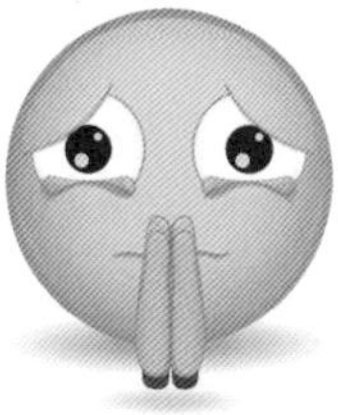

L

M

N

O

P

_____ 1. Do you want to fight?
_____ 2. I'm in a hurry!
_____ 3. Go away!
_____ 4. I'm tired.
_____ 5. Stop!
_____ 6. I'm so sorry.
_____ 7. It stinks.*
_____ 8. I love you.
_____ 9. I don't know.
_____ 10. I'm scared.
_____ 11. Hey, wait for me!
_____ 12. I'm depressed.*
_____ 13. Yuck!*
_____ 14. It's hot.
_____ 15. Yay!
_____ 16. Good job!*

*stink 臭う　　depressed 落ち込んだ　　yuck! ゲー！　　good job! よくやったね！

6 Activity: How Many Triangles? アクティビティ：三角形はいくつある?

How many triangles can you find in the shape below? Write your total in the space below.
下の絵にはいくつの三角形がありますか?

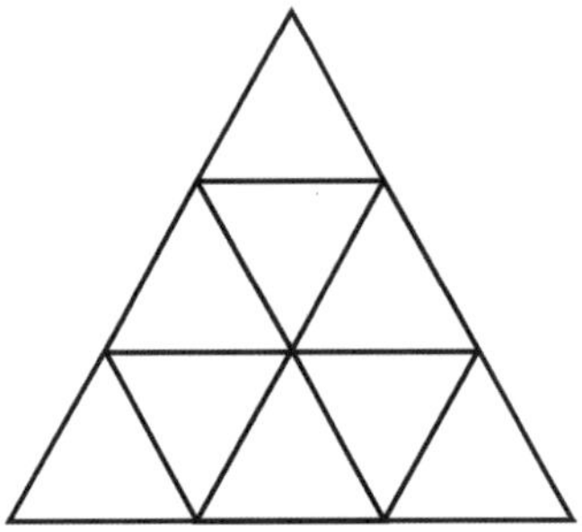

There are ________ triangles.

7 Case Study: The Gesture ケーススタディ：ジェスチャー

After a business meeting at a Japanese company, a visiting American businessman was taken to a taxi, which then drove him to the nearest train station. When the foreigner climbed out of the taxi, the Japanese taxi driver gestured to the American, making a circle with his thumb and forefinger.

The American replied, "Oh, I see. Thank you!" and walked away. The taxi driver was surprised and unhappy.

Question: What was the cause of this miscommunication?

8 Activity: Mime Activity アクティビティ：ジェスチャーゲーム

Your teacher will give you some words for you to act out nonverbally.
Try your best and have fun!
感情を表す表現を、ことばを使わずに体や表情を使って表してみましょう。
楽しみながらゲーム感覚でやってみましょう。

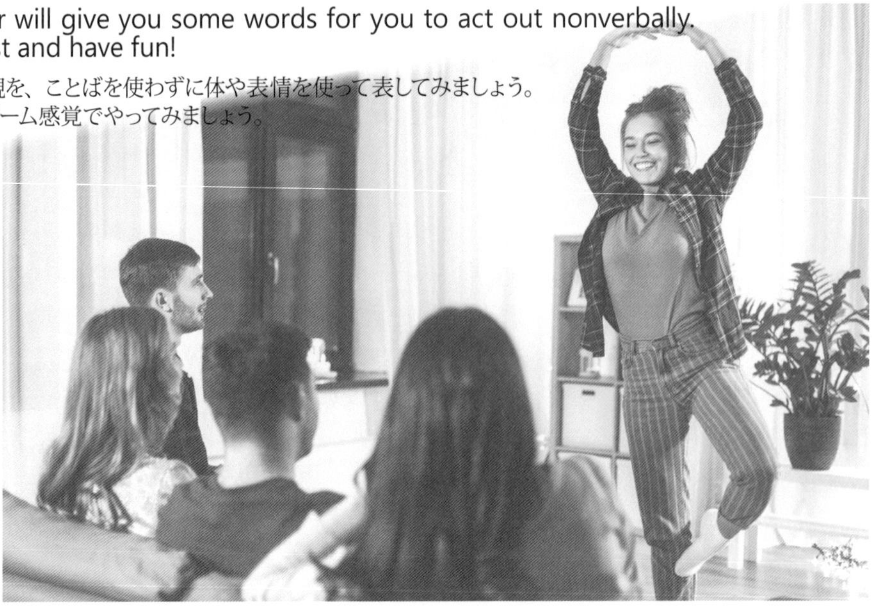

9 Discussion: English as a Design

ディスカッション：デザインとしての英語

Many foreigners enjoy reading "Jap-lish."

Questions:

Look at the picture above. Why do many Japanese like to have English on their T-shirts, shopping bags, and other things? Why is the English often strange?

上の絵を見てください。日本人はなぜ英語が書かれたTシャツや紙袋などを好むのでしょうか？　なぜこれらの英語は不自然なことが多いのでしょうか？

Look for English in the environment around you and write down four words, expressions or sentences that you see. The English could be on a train, on a T-shirt, on a poster, a shopping bag, or other places.

あなたのまわりにある英語の言葉、文、表現を探してみましょう。電車の中、Tシャツ、ポスター、紙袋など、様々な場所に見つかるはずです。

1. ______________________________
2. ______________________________
3. ______________________________
4. ______________________________

10 Case Study: The International Party

ケーススタディ：国際パーティ

A Japanese young woman was at an international party and met a young man from Brazil. While they were talking, the Brazilian tried to step closer to the Japanese woman. She backed away each time until she was up against the wall. She was very uncomfortable.

Question: What is the cause of this problem?

11 Activity: Company Logos

アクティビティ：会社のロゴ

Companies spend a lot of money to design their logos, and they often have special meaning. Look at the logos in Appendix 5 on page 104 and answer the questions below.

会社は、特別な意味を持たせた自社のロゴをデザインするために莫大な費用を使います。Appendix 5（p.104）を見て以下の質問に答えましょう。

A.

1. What is the name of the company? ______________________

2. Can you see the hidden symbol in this logo? What does this symbol mean?

____

3. What do the three colors (including the white background) represent?

____

B.

1. What is this the flag for? ______________________
2. Why are there five rings? ______________________
3. Why are the circles overlapping? ______________________
4. Why are there six colors (including the white background)? ______________________

C.

1. What company uses this emoji? ______________________
2. What does it mean? ______________________

D.

1. What company uses this logo? ______________________
2. What does the logo mean? ______________________
3. How does the logo relate to the name of the company? ______________________

E.

1. What company uses this logo? ______________________

2. What is the woman in the picture and what is she holding in her hands?

____

3. What meaning does this symbol have? ______________________

Unit 7
Values
価値観

1 Pair Work: Values in Advertising

ペアワーク：広告に見る価値観

Many advertisements have social messages. Sometimes these social ads ask you to think more about your values, to consider changing your behavior, or to take action to do something for others. Work in pairs. Look at the ads in Appendix 6A, 6B, and 6C on pages 105 to 107 and answer the questions below.

多くの広告は社会的なメッセージを発信しています。これらの広告によって、私たちは自分の価値観について深く考えたり、行動を変えたり、周りの人たちのために何かしようと行動を起こすこともあります。パートナーといっしょに Appendix 6A、6B、6C（p.104 ～ p.107）の広告を見て、以下の質問に答えましょう。

A.

1. What is the target market of this ad? ______________________________
2. How does the picture relate to the headline? ______________________________
3. What does the ad ask readers to do? ______________________________
4. Is this ad effective? Why or why not? ______________________________

B.

1. What is the target market of this ad? ______________________________
2. How does the picture relate to the headline? ______________________________
3. What does the ad ask readers to do? ______________________________
4. Is this ad effective? Why or why not? ______________________________

C.

1. What is the target market of this ad? ______________________________
2. How does the picture relate to the headline? ______________________________
3. What does the ad ask readers to do? ______________________________
4. Is this ad effective? Why or why not? ______________________________

2 Group Activity: The Story of Juliet

17

グループアクティビティ：ジュリエットのストーリー

Read the following story. After you have finished, discuss the five people in the story. In a group, give each person a number, from #1 (the best person) to #5 (the worst person). Be prepared to tell the class why you made your choices.

以下のストーリーを読み終わったら、登場人物５人について話し合いましょう。登場人物の中で最もよい人（No.1）から最も悪い人（No.5）まで番号を付けましょう。そしてなぜそう思うのかをクラスメイトに説明しましょう。

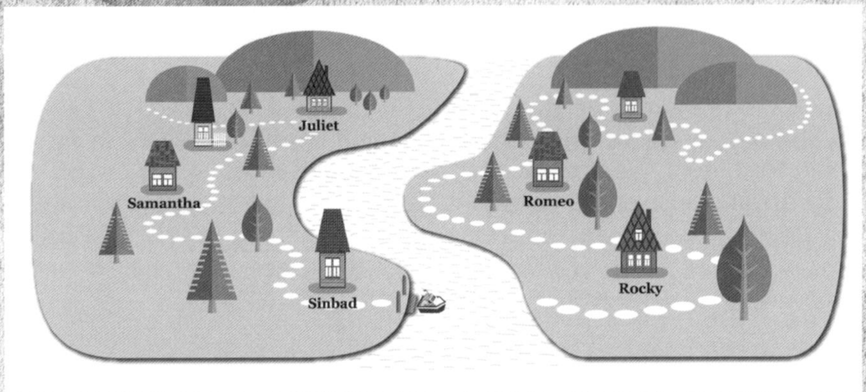

Once upon a time, there was a woman named Juliet who lived in a village near a river. She was very much in love with Romeo, who lived in the village across the river. It was difficult to get across the river, especially in the winter when there was a lot of water.

Juliet wanted to be with Romeo so much. One winter, she went to a man named Sinbad, who had the only boat in the village. She asked him to take her across the river. Sinbad said, "Yes, but you must pay me $500." "That's ten times your normal price. I don't have that much money!" Juliet shouted. "That's too bad. You really want to be with Romeo, right?" Sinbad laughed.

She then went to her best friend's house, Samantha, and told her what happened. Samantha said, "I don't want to hear about this and I'm not going to loan you any money. Solve your problems by yourself." Juliet was sad and left.

After crying for several hours, Juliet stole $500 from a rich neighbor and promised herself she would pay it back later. She gave the money to Sinbad, who then took her across the river. Juliet arrived at Romeo's house and they hugged. "By the way," Romeo asked, "how did you get across the river?" Juliet explained honestly, and Romeo became angry. "You're a thief! Go away! I never want to see you again!" he shouted. Juliet left in tears.

She went to another friend's house, a man named Rocky, and told him the whole story.

"I'm going to go to Romeo's house and beat him up*," said Rocky. When he came back to his house, he told Juliet that Romeo was now in the hospital. He also said, "I don't really love you, Juliet, but I'll marry you if you want."

-The End-

*beat up　殴り倒す

Character	Positive value(s)	Negative value(s)
1.		
2.		
3.		
4.		
5.		

3 Pair work: Rules for the World

ペアワーク：世の中のルールをつくる

Imagine you have the power to make three rules that everyone in the world must follow. What would those rules be?

世界中の人が従わなくてはならないルールを３つ作れるとしたら、どんなルールを作りますか?

Rule #1: ______________________________

Rule #2: ______________________________

Rule #3: ______________________________

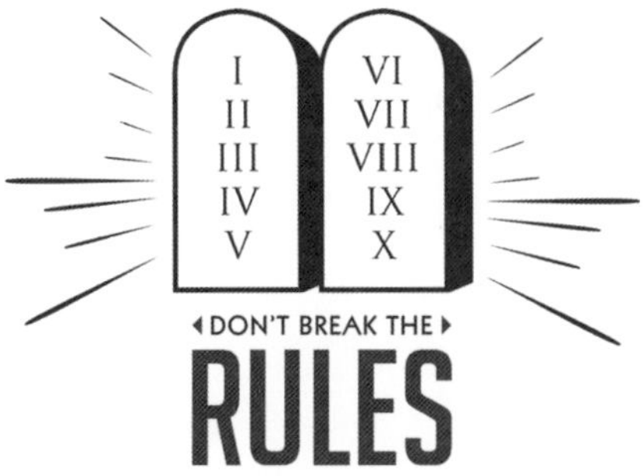

4 Group Activity: The Fire

グループアクティビティ：火事

A tall skyscraper* is on fire, and 12 people are trapped* on the 40th floor. One elevator is ready to leave, but it can hold only eight people. The others will likely not make it to safety. The 12 people are:

_____ 1. A male 58-year-old priest* who does a lot of community work for the poor.

_____ 2. A 64-year-old male company president whose wife died of cancer last year.

_____ 3. A 46-year-old male doctor who is a famous heart surgeon* for children.

_____ 4. A 47-year-old female politician active in the environment and climate-change prevention.

_____ 5. A 17-year-old female high-school student who just became a single mother.

_____ 6. A 31-year-old female journalist who just won an award for exposing* political corruption*.

_____ 7. A 59-year-old farmer who invented a better way to grow vegetables all year round.

_____ 8. A 28-year-old former drug abuser* who is now a counselor for young drug abusers.

_____ 9. A 48-year-old female economics professor and mother of three young children.

_____ 10. A 27-year-old female professional tennis player who is a millionaire.

_____ 11. A 29-year-old male rock musician who takes drugs and has attempted suicide* twice.

_____ 12. A 34-year-old male police officer with a young daughter.

First, decide who should go on the elevator by numbering your choices from 1 (first person you want saved) to number 8 (last person you want saved). Then work in a group and come to a consensus on who should be saved. Be prepared to share your logic.

*skyscraper 超高層ビル
trap 閉じ込める
priest 神父
heart surgeon 心臓外科医
expose 暴露する
political corruption 政治的な汚職
drug abuser 薬物乱用者
attempted suicide 自殺未遂

5 Pair Work: Foreigners in Japan ペアワーク：日本の外国人

What do you think the following pictures show in terms of value differences?
以下の絵が表す価値観の違いについて、どう思いますか？

1

Foreigners are surprised by Japanese noodle-eating manners.

2

Foreign men are shocked to see cleaning ladies in the restroom.

3

Foreigners are surprised that students clean their classrooms and toilets.

4

5

Foreigners are sometimes surprised by what Japanese children get away with.

6

7

Many Foreigners can't understand why Japanese don't protest against the "noise invasion."

6 Group Activity: Stereotypes about Japanese

グループアクティビティ：日本人に関するステレオタイプ

Page 55 and 56 show stereotypes and ideas that some people from other countries may have about Japanese. In groups of three, choose three stereotypes and talk about why people may have these ideas. Share your own ideas about what is true. When you are done, give a short talk about the stereotypes. Imagine you are talking to foreigners who have little knowledge about Japan. Be prepared to give details about Japanese people so that the non-Japanese listeners have a deeper understanding.

1. Japanese are workaholics.

2. Japan is a man's country. Japanese women are obedient* to men.

3. Japanese are shy.

4. Japanese are formal.

5. Japanese are always in groups and they feel comfortable when they follow the group way.

6. Japanese are "two-faced." They do not show their true feelings.

7. Japanese are "nerdy" or "geeky.*" They are smart and like animation and computer games.

8. Japanese women like to wear kimono.

9. Most Japanese are good at karate and other martial arts.*

*obedient 従順な　geeky オタクの　martial arts 武道

7 Case Study: The Factory ケーススタディ：工場

18

A Japanese company is building a factory in a town in Mexico. There have been several delays, and now the factory completion date is behind schedule*. The Japanese director in Mexico offered workers extra money to work evenings, weekends, and holidays, but most of the workers said they were not interested in working overtime, even though the pay for extra work was higher than normal. The director scolded* the workers for their laziness*, explaining to them that men "live to work" and told them they lacked* loyalty* to the company.

*behind schedule 予定より遅れて　scold しかる　laziness 怠惰さ　lack 足りない　loyalty 忠誠心

Questions:

1. Why did the workers refuse overtime work?
2. What does this show about their values? About Japanese values?

Unit 8

Creative Thinking

独創的思考

1 Group Activity: Designing a Paper Airplane

グループアクティビティ：紙飛行機をデザインする

In this activity you will need to think creatively and come up with practical, effective ideas. You and your team will be given paper to make paper airplanes. Your goal is to make planes that can fly a long distance. You will have about ten minutes to strategize and make your airplanes. Then you will compete with the other teams to see which paper airplanes fly the best.

このアクティビティでは、創造力を駆使して効果的なアイデアを考えなければなりません。チームごとに紙飛行機を作るために紙が配られます。目標は飛距離の長い紙飛行機を作ることです。10 分で考え紙飛行機を作ってください。作り終えたら、どのチームの飛行機が一番長く飛ばせるかを競いましょう。

2 Activity: Analyzing Advertisements

アクティビティ：広告を分析する

Look at the product advertisements in Appendix 7A, 7B, and 7C on pages 108 and 109, and answer the following questions.

Appendix 7A、7B、7C（p.108 ～ p.109）の商品の広告を見て、以下の質問に答えましょう。

A.

1. What is the product? ______________________________

2. How do the headline and visual work together? ______________________________

____

3. What are the main benefits of this insurance policy?* ______________________________

____

4. Who is the target market? ______________________________

*insurance policy 保険契約

B.

1. What is the product? ______________________________

2. How do the headline and visuals work together? ______________________________

____

3. What is the main benefit? The secondary benefit? ____________________

____

4. Who is the main target market? ____________________
5. What kind of media or publication* would be suitable* for this ad?____________________

____

*publication 出版物　　suitable 適切な

C.
1. What is the product? ____________________
2. What is the main benefit mentioned? A secondary benefit? ____________________

____

3. Who is the target market? ____________________
4. What kind of media or publication would be suitable for this ad? ____________________

____

3 Case Study: Creativity and Culture

ケーススタディ：クリエイティビティと文化

Sometimes an idea that is successful in one culture may not be successful in another. In groups, discuss why the following three international ad campaigns failed in certain countries. Why were they unsuccessful in those countries?

ある文化にとって適切なアイデアでも、ほかの文化にとって不適切とみなされることもあります。他の国での３つの国際的な広告のキャンペーンについて話し合いましょう。なぜ成功しなかったのでしょう？　以下の広告や商品名は、どの国で問題となったのでしょうか？

Ad #1

An advertisement for an international airline aimed to show how wonderful their first-class service was. The ad showed a flight attendant giving champagne to an invisible* passenger who is wearing headphones while enjoying a wonderful meal sitting in his first-class seat. The headline was "Put yourself in our place! Enjoy Southeast Airline's First-Class service." The ad was successful in Japan, but not in Korea and China. Why?

*invisible 透明な

Notes: ____________________

____

____

Ad #2

A travel company shows a happy, loving young couple at a beach in a tropical paradise. The aim of the ad was to increase travel to some islands. The advertisement was successful in Japan and the U.S., but not in some other countries. Which countries did not like the ad? Why?

Notes:

Ad #3

An American automobile company made a new line of cars, which they named "Nova." The cars sold poorly in countries in Central America and South America. Why?

Notes:

4 Activity: Invention アクティビティ：発明

Think of two new products or services that you think would be popular and would make a good business opportunity. Write a description of the products or services below. You may also want to draw a picture of your invention to help explain it to a group of other students.

ビジネスチャンスのありそうな商品、サービスを２つ考えてください。その内容を以下に書いて、クラスメイトに説明しましょう。

1.	2.

Present your ideas to a group of students.

5 Pair Work: Advertising Campaign

ペアワーク：広告キャンペーン

Choose one of the product or service ideas from Activity 4 and prepare a marketing plan. Here are the steps you need to consider:

アクティビティ４で考えた商品、サービスからひとつ選び、以下の項目を考慮してマーケティングの方法を考えてください。

1. What benefits does the product offer to buyers and users?
2. Who would the buyers (the target market) likely be?
3. What is the competition? What can you offer that the competition does not?
4. Give a name to your product. You may want to think about what image you would like your product to have, since naming and imaging sometimes go together.
5. Prepare an ad for the product with a picture, a headline, and body copy. Instead of print advertising, you may choose to write and prepare a TV commercial.
6. Present your product idea and advertisement to the class. Talk about points 1 to 4 above during your presentation.

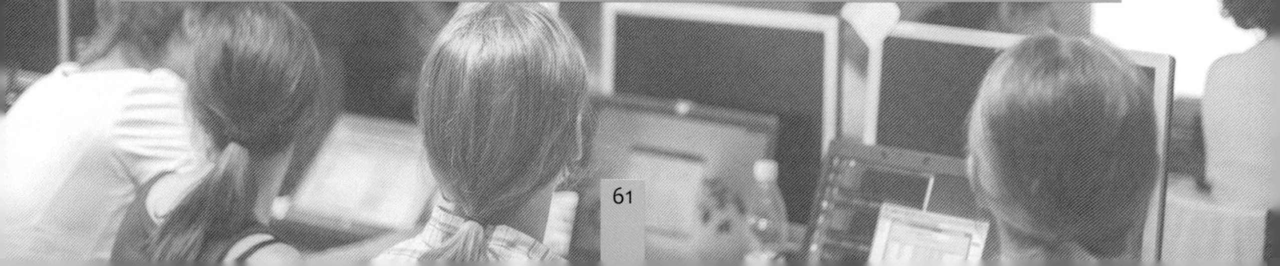

6 Group Discussion: Creativity

グループディスカッション：クリエイティビティ

Questions:

1. Are you creative? How do you show your creativity?

2. Would you like to become more creative? How would you like to express your creativity?

3. Does the Japanese educational system encourage creativity in students?

7 Original Activities

オリジナルアクティビティ

Design your own case study or activity to present to the class. You can look at the activities in the textbook to get ideas. First, brainstorm several ideas and present them to a group. Then select the most interesting one and prepare the activity (with illustrations and other items, if necessary). Your instructor will check the activity before you present it.

自分でケーススタディやアクティビティを考え、クラスで発表します。テキスト内のアクティビティをヒントにしても OK です。まずアイデアがいくつか出たらグループ内で話し合い、最もおもしろいものをひとつ選びましょう。必要ならイラストや写真なども使って発表してください。発表する前に先生にチェックしてもらいましょう。

8 Pair Work: Funnies

ペアワーク：1 コマ漫画

Choose some cartoons in Appendix 8A to 8O on pages 110 and 111 and write something funny or interesting in the speech balloons. After you have finished, share them in groups.

Appendix 8 の 8A ～ 8O（p.110、p.111）の絵の中から好きなものをいくつか選び、吹き出しの中に楽しいセリフを入れましょう。書き終わったらグループ内でシェアしてください。

Unit 9

Business

ビジネス

1 Case Study: The Negotiation ケーススタディ：交渉

A Brazilian company was interested in selling the products of a Swiss Company in Brazil. The Swiss salesman had carefully prepared for the meeting and was ready to offer what he believed to be a good deal* to the Brazilian. He made a PowerPoint presentation with many statistics* to prove his point. They sat down in a conference room and, after quick introductions, the Swiss began negotiations. After all, he did not have time to waste. For some reason, the Brazilian did not seem comfortable or friendly and he stopped the negotiations in the middle of discussion, telling the Swiss he was no longer interested in doing business with him. The Swiss was shocked, believing that his offer was more than fair and that the Brazilian could make a good profit.

*good deal 得な取引　　statistics 統計データ

2 Case Study: The Disagreement ケーススタディ：意見の対立

An American in Japan was having a disagreement with a Japanese business colleague working in the same office (both are managers). He believed that the Japanese businessman should have consulted him about concluding a contract he was involved in. The American was quite angry and wanted to settle* this problem so that future problems could be avoided. The Japanese colleague did not speak much or answer questions directly. Instead, he said things like, "Let's just calm down*." He also smiled and laughed. This made the American even angrier because he felt the Japanese was laughing at him and not taking the situation seriously.

*settle 解決する　　calm down 落ち着く

Questions:

1 Why might the American have misunderstood the Japanese colleague's cues?*

2. Why didn't the Japanese colleague want to "talk things out"?

*cue 合図

3 Case Study: The Promotion　ケーススタディ：昇進

An American was teaching English at a large English-language school in Tokyo for Japanese business executives. His contract* was for one year, which could be renewed* each year. The president of the company appointed* him to the position of personnel manager* and told him that, in addition to his new duties*, he must continue teaching his 15 classes each week. He was popular with his client companies.

The teacher was surprised about the work conditions and knew he would have a lot of overtime*, sometimes 20 hours a week of overtime. He asked what his new salary would be.

"Same as your salary now," answered the president. The American was now shocked. He talked to a Japanese employee of the same company, who told him, "Your reward* is to be appreciated by the company. It could be good for your future."

"But I'm a contract worker with a one-year renewable* contract," the American replied. "I don't know what my long-term future at this company will be."

*contract 契約　renew 更新する　appoint 任命する　personnel manager 人事課長
duty 任務、責務　overtime 残業　reward 報酬　renewable 更新可能な

Questions:

1. Do you think the job offer was good for the American? Why or why not?
2. What would Japanese workers do in this situation?

4 Case Study: Job Interview　ケーススタディ：就職の面接

The president of a Japanese private university* met with a British candidate* for professor* at the university. The candidate passed two interviews and had an excellent resume. The president asked him to sign a contract for the position, but the contract was incomplete.* The information about salary was missing. The British teacher said that he felt uncomfortable signing an incomplete contract.

The president told him he didn't have to sign the contract, but as soon as the candidate was out of the room, he told his staff not to hire* the candidate.

*private university 私立大学　candidate 候補者　professor 教授
incomplete 不完全な　hire 採用する

Questions:

1. Why was the president against the candidate?
2. Should the candidate have signed the contract right away?
3. Why do you think the candidate was reluctant* to sign?

*reluctant 気乗りしない

5 Pair Work: Business Opportunity

ペアワーク：ビジネスチャンス

Work in pairs. You plan to open a new retail store. First, decide whether you want a restaurant or store selling products or services. Profit is an important goal. When ready, fill out the information below.

ペアになって新しいお店を開く計画を立てましょう。まずどのようなサービス / 商品を提供する店かを決めてください。利益を出すことが重要な目的です。準備ができたら情報を書き入れましょう。

Name of store / restaurant	
Location	
Target market	

For Store

1. What kind of products or services will you sell? ______________________
2. Who is your target market? ______________________
3. How did you choose your location? ______________________
4. What are the benefits of your products / services? ______________________
5. What are your major expenses? How can you limit these expenses?

____

6. How can you reach out to your customers (advertising, promotion, internet, etc.)?

____

For Restaurant

1. What kind of food will you offer? What is unique or attractive about your menu?

____

2. Who is your target market? ______________________
3. How did you choose your location? ______________________
4. How big will your store be? How many employees will you have?

____

5. What are your major expenses? How can you limit these expenses?

____

6. How can you reach out to your customers (advertising, promotion, internet, etc.)?

____

6 Reading: Business Email リーディング：ビジネスメール

American office workers receive over 80 email a day on average.* People don't have time to read all of them. Therefore, when writing an email, it's important to be clear and keep your email short. Writers of business email should:

1 Keep in mind* who you are writing to and what that person knows. Include only information that is important or interesting to that person.

2 When addressing* the message, keep in mind the purpose of "To" and "Cc."

To: The main target for your email and those people who you hope will take an action or reply to your message.

CC: People you hope will see the message but who do not need to reply or take an action.

3 After "Subject*", write the purpose of the email. Make it clear and short, but be sure to include the main theme* of the message. Try to make the message specific* and clear.

Good examples:

Subject: Your copy machine order of November 2nd

Subject: Your conference presentation on March 3rd

Bad Examples:

Subject: Important!

Subject: For your information

4 A greeting and a friendly opening sentence are important to make a connection or show appreciation.

Greetings:

Dear Mr. Markle: (formal)

Dear Cindy, (informal)

Friendly openings:

I appreciate the time and effort you have given to help me with this project.

It was wonderful meeting you at the job fair last Friday.

Thank you for your email.

5 The best emails have just one important message. If the message requires more information or steps, then use numbers to make it simple and clear. A good example:

1. Please check the English in the Sales Report.
2. Make sure the information is correct.
3. Add the sales data you have for this month. Graphs and tables would be helpful.
4. Send it back to me by Friday, April 30th.

6 Call to action* and close: A good email tells the reader what action you want them to take, usually at the end of the email.

Good example:

I would appreciate an opportunity to meet you at your office next week, if possible. Please let me know the day and time you are available.*

*on average 平均して　keep in mind 覚えておく　address 宛名を書く
subject 件名　theme テーマ、主題　specific 明確な　call to action 行動を要請
available（人が）会うことができる、（予定が）空いている

True or False 内容把握

Write "T" if the sentence is true or "F" if it is false.
内容と一致している場合は "T" を、一致していなければ "F" を入れましょう。

_____ 1. It is a good idea to include information in your email that the reader already knows in order to avoid mistakes.

_____ 2. The names you put after "CC" are people you hope will take an action based on your email.

_____ 3. The specific purpose of the email should be stated after "Subject".

_____ 4. It is a good idea to include a friendly sentence at the beginning of your email to better connect with the reader.

_____ 5. You should include all important messages you can think of in one email to avoid sending too many email.

_____ 6. It is important to have a call to action if you want the reader to do something, usually near the end of your email.

7 Activity: Business Email アクティビティ：ビジネスメール

Circle the letter (A, B, or C) of the most effective email among the following.
以下のメールの中で最も効果的なメールの記号を◯で囲みましょう。

A.

To:	jedwards@gmail.com
CC:	msuzuki@hotmail.co.jp
Subject:	Resume received

Dear Mr. Edwards:

We received your resume* on April 16th. Thank you for your interest in the marketing manager position at ReMax Corporation. We have forwarded* your resume to the Marketing and Sales Department for their review*. If your skills, background*, and education match the requirements* of the current* position, we will contact you to schedule an interview. If you are not selected for an interview at this time, please know we will keep your resume on file for one year in case we have another opening that better matches your experience.

Again, thank you for your interest in working for ReMax. We wish you all the best in your job search.

Sincerely,
Candice Berger, Human Relations Director

*resume 履歴書　forward 転送する　review 検討　background 経歴　requirement 必要条件　current 現在の

B.

To:	AWilliams@gmail.com
CC:	
Subject:	Urgent*!!! Important Business Offer!!!

Dear Mr. Williams:

I found your name and email in the city's list of shop owners in the greater Boston area and thought you'd be interested in what I can offer you. I'm an advertising and marketing specialist. I also have experience in sales promotion and have a lot of great ideas. I really feel I can be of service to you.

BTW, I have been involved in* assisting retail* businesses in different ways for over 25 years. Please contact me if you think I can help you in any way. You won't be sorry.

I look forward to hearing from you soon!!!

Sincerely,
Maxwell Rigby, Consultant

*urgent 緊急の　be involved in ~ ～に関与する　retail 小売りの

C.

To:	ZachT@gmail.com
CC:	BernieS@speedmail.co.jp
Subject:	Greetings

Dear Ms. Tolleson:

Thank you for choosing our company to provide you with your business needs. I am sure you will be happy with the services that we offer in the years ahead. In the attachment*, you will find detailed* information about the services we provide* as well as contact information. We hope you find this information useful. After reading our service brochure*, feel free to call us if you have any questions.

For your information, your account number* is CZ4263F. Please have this number handy if you call us with any requests so we can expedite* the requested service.

As your needs change in the future, you may find that your requirements from us may change. In such a case, we will be happy to work with you to determine* how best we can be of service to you so you can achieve* your goals.

Again, we appreciate that you chose TrenTex to meet your current and future needs.

Sincerely,
Patrick Harper, Sales Director

*attachment 添付　detailed 詳細の　provide 提供する　brochure パンフレット
account number 顧客番号　expedite 迅速に処理する　determine 決める　achieve 達成する

8 Writing: Business Email

ライティング：ビジネスメール

Choose one of the situations below and write your own email.
以下の状況から一つ選んで、ビジネスメールを書いてみましょう。

1 You are a third-year student in economics* with the second-highest grade point average* in your class. It is April and you write to the personnel department* of a well-known financial services company to ask if you can serve as an intern in their summer internship program this year. You write to Paula Langdon, Manager of Human Resources* at Finley Financial Services. You got her name and contact information from a senior at your university who was an intern at Finley Financial Services last summer and who was recently offered a full-time job at the company. The senior, Justin Tremont, said he would be happy to recommend you for an intern position.

2 You are a new college graduate. You just had a job interview at Techtron, a high-technology company, and you hope to be hired. You forgot to tell the interviewer*, Jenna Jones, Manager of Human Resources, that you were president of the computer club at your university, and that club members developed a new, successful social networking site for university students.

3 You ordered a pair of shoes from a network site called Shoesational and discover that one shoe is size seven and the other is size seven and a half. The size seven fits perfectly. You want to know whether you should return both shoes or just the one shoe. You also want to ask them whether the network sales company will reimburse* you for shipping expenses*. You feel they should, since it was their mistake.

4 You want to ask a professor, Julia Sanders, at your former university, the University of California, Santa Barbara, for a recommendation* for a job at a major* Japanese bank. You received an "A" in the professor's class in Economics 301, and the professor was your advisor for your graduation thesis titled, "The Role of American Banks in the Recession* of 2008," for which you also received an "A". You hope the professor will also mention that you had the highest GPA for your class during your senior (4th) year and were given an award for "Outstanding* Student of the Year" at the university.

*economics 経済学　grade point average (GPA) 成績平均点
personnel department 人事部　Human Resources 人事　interviewer 面接官
reimburse 払戻す　shipping expenses 配送料　recommendation 推薦
major 大手の　recession 不況　outstanding きわめて優れた

Your Email

To:	
CC:	
Subject:	

Dear ____________________:

Unit 10

Personal Issues

個人的なこと

1 Writing: Smartphone Problem

ライティング：スマホ問題

Read the following email written to a newspaper columnist asking for advice. Imagine you are Dana (the columnist) and write an answer.

以下は、新聞のコラムニスト、Danaにアドバイスを求めるメールです。自分がDanaだったらメールにどう答えますか？

Dear Dana,

I bought a smartphone for my daughter, Cindy, when she was 12 years old. Her school recommended that we get her a smartphone because homework assignments and notes from the school are often posted on the internet. Cindy's now 14 years old and is on her smartphone day and night. She used to be very active, playing outside or meeting friends in the neighborhood. Now, she spends most of her time playing games on her smartphone or looking at social networking sites in her bedroom. I often tell her to put it away during dinnertime, when she's working on her homework, or when she's doing other activities. However, she gets angry whenever I try to limit her smartphone use.

Now she has a bigger problem. She's become depressed the last few months and often stays in her room alone. Her grades are getting worse and she doesn't seem to care. I have no idea what I should do. Dana, please help!*

Sincerely, Worried Mother!

*depressed 落ち込んだ

Dear Worried Mother,

Sincerely, Dana

Share your answer with a group. Who do you think has the best advice?

グループ内で答えをシェアしましょう。誰のアドバイスが一番適切だと思いますか？

2 Writing: Marital Problem

ライティング：結婚問題

Read the following email written to a newspaper columnist asking for advice. Imagine you are Dana and write an answer.

以下は、新聞のコラムニスト、Danaにアドバイスを求めるメールです。自分がDanaだったらメールにどう答えますか？

Dear Dana:

I am Japanese. I married a man from Peru named Juan five years ago, and we live in Japan. I graduated from college, but he didn't. We now have two children. Juan works as a carpenter, and his salary is rather* low. I want to work also, but he refuses* to let me. Moreover, he's out most weekends with his friends, often playing soccer. I sometimes want him to stay home with the children so I can go out and meet my friends, but he tells me I'm selfish and I should think more about the family's needs. What should I do?*

From Frustrated Wife*

*carpenter 大工　rather かなり　refuse 拒否する　frustrated イライラしている

Dear Frustrated Wife,

Sincerely, Dana

Share your answer with a group. Who do you think has the best advice?

グループ内で答えをシェアしましょう。誰のアドバイスが一番適切だと思いますか？

3 Activity: Life Partner アクティビティ：人生のパートナー

What are the important characteristics of an ideal partner for you? Mark your choices by writing 1 to 14 below. Write "1" for most important, "2" for second most important, etcetera.

あなたの理想のパートナーに求める資質とは何ですか？　一番重要なポイントには "1" を、2 番目に重要なポイントには "2"、というように、優先順位を書き入れてみましょう。

Characteristics	Your Choice	Team Choice
Well educated		
Attractive		
Similar age		
Honest and trustworthy		
Funny		
Wealthy		
Friendly and outgoing		
Loyal		
Healthy		
Has similar interests and likes		
A good listener, patient, and sensitive		
Ambitious and hard working		
Knowledgeable and intelligent		
Other:		

Now, in a group, decide the most important points and characteristics. Write 1 to 14 in the "Team Choice" boxes, with one being the most important.

さあ、今度はグループのメンバーと話し合って、最も重要な資質を選び、"Team Choice" に 1 から 14 まで優先順位を付けてみましょう。

4 Activity: Day-to-Day Stress アクティビティ：日々のストレス

First, write down five things that cause stress in your life (e.g. homework, parents, future planning, money, etc.).

生活の中で最もストレスを感じさせることは何ですか？　５つ選んで書いてみましょう。（宿題、両親、将来についてなど）

1. ______________________________
2. ______________________________
3. ______________________________
4. ______________________________
5. ______________________________

Next, in a group, decide the top three things that cause the most stress. Why are these things so stressful?

次にグループ内で、最もストレスを感じることを３つ選んでください。選んだ理由も書いてみましょう。

	Group's Most Stressful Things	Reasons Why
1.		
2.		
3.		

5 Case Study: Culture Shock

28

ケーススタディ：カルチャーショック

The Social Readjustment Rating Scale* shows the amount of stress we feel from different life changes. The stress from these events lasts for about six months. If you have several changes, the stress adds up. When we move to a foreign country, we go through many life changes and our stress usually increases.

Read the case of Mark Sherman and decide which events and stresses he is experiencing. The list on page 77 is not complete: there would be even more changes and stress from a move abroad. But it does give you some idea about the stress caused by moving overseas.

Case study:

Mark Sherman moved to Tokyo from the U.S. His family will join him in five months. He was given a new position, director, at his company. His house is far from his work, so he must get up early. His salary is now much higher, but he has a lot of overtime work. He calls his wife every day, but recently, they have been arguing on the phone about different things. Mark gets angry more often. He is lonely on his days off because he can no longer meet his family, including his parents. He also cannot meet his old friends and he no longer feels like playing tennis, which he used to play with friends. He also doesn't go to church, which he used to do in the U.S. He is getting thinner* because he often doesn't feel like eating by himself.

*Social Readjustment Rating Scale (SRRS) 社会的再適応評価尺度　　thinner より痩せた

Challenge

Look at the stress chart on page 77, put the stress scores for the stress events Mark Sherman is experiencing (one has been done for you), then add them up for the total stress score. How much stress does he have?

77ページのストレスチャートを見て、Mark Shermanが経験している出来事のストレス度を測ってみましょう（ひとつは既に記載されています）、その後ストレス度の数値を合計してみましょう。彼はどのくらいのストレスを抱えていますか?

	Life Changes	Average Stress Score	Mark's Stress
1.	Death of spouse*	100	
2.	Divorce*	73	
3.	Separated from wife or husband	65	
4.	Death of close family member	63	
5.	Marriage	50	
6.	Fired* from job	47	
7.	Retirement*	45	
8.	Major change in work	39	
9.	Change in finances (salary, etc.)	38	
10.	Change to a different type of work	36	
11.	Change in number of arguments with husband or wife	35	
12.	Change in responsibilities at work	26	
13.	Change in living conditions	25	
14.	Change in personal habits*	24	
15.	Change in work hours or conditions	20	
16.	Moving to a new house	20	20
17.	Change in recreation*	19	
18.	Change in church activities	19	
19.	Change in social activities	18	
20.	Change in sleeping habits	16	
21.	Change in number of family get-togethers	15	
22.	Change in eating habits	15	

Total stress score for Mark Sherman ______

*spouse 配偶者　divorce 離婚（する）　fire 解雇する
retirement 退職　habit 習慣　recreation 娯楽

6 Case Study: The Note ケーススタディ：メモ書き

A Japanese girl name Mia lived in Hong Kong for eight years, where she attended an international school. Her friends and classmates were mainly American, so she became rather Americanized*— open and assertive*. She spoke English like a native speaker. She returned to Japan with her family and attended a Japanese high school. During class, she would often raise her hand when she knew the answers and she was sometimes blunt* with her friends.

Soon, she was bullied* and was getting negative postings on her social networking site. One student gave her a note that said, “No one likes you. You should quit this school!” She cried and went to her homeroom teacher to show the note. The teacher told Mia, “I understand how your classmates feel. You’re not like a normal Japanese. You think you’re better than other people.”

Mia went home and thought about ending her life. Fortunately, her grandmother returned home and talked her out of hurting herself. Years later, Mia is in university and is much stronger and happier. She decided that she wants to help young returnees* adjust* to life in Japan.

*Americanized アメリカナイズされた　assertive 自己主張する　blunt ぶっきらぼうな
bullied いじめられる　returnee 帰国子女　adjust 適応する

Questions:

1. Why did Mia have adjustment problems in Japan?
2. What should the homeroom teacher have said or done?
3. What could Mia have done differently to avoid or solve her problems?
4. How can schools prepare to help returnees and foreigners with their special problems?

7 Group Work: Personal Goal グループワーク：自分のゴール

Look back to Activity 7 of Unit 3 on page 26. How successful were you in reaching your goal or taking steps to reach your goal? What helped you or what prevented you from reaching your goal? Be prepared to talk about your goal in a group.

Activity 7の Unit 3 (p.26) を見てください。自分のゴールを達成できていますか？　達成するためのステップを踏み出しましたか？

8 Activity: To Tell the Truth

アクティビティ：本当のはなし

First, write about an interesting experience you had, for example, a place you visited, a famous person you saw, or an accident you had. Write one or two sentences.

自分のユニークな経験（訪れた場所、会ったことのある有名人、事故や記憶に残る出来事など）について書きましょう。

Interesting experience: ______________________________

____

____

____

____

Share your story with other students in your group. The group should then choose the most interesting one. All members in your group will stand in front of the class and share a similar story, but only one person is telling the truth. The class will ask questions to see who is telling the truth. Have fun!

自分のストーリーを同じグループ内の人とシェアし、最も興味深いストーリーを選んでください。そのグループのメンバーはクラスメイトの前で、同じようなストーリーをシェアします。でも本当のことを言っているのはひとりだけです。誰が真実を語っているか、当てましょう。

Example:

Student A: "I ate horsemeat* in Nagano. It was delicious." (not true)
Student B: "I ate horsemeat in Hokkaido. It was raw, and I didn't like it." (not true)
Student C: "I ate horsemeat at a restaurant in Tokyo. It was terrible.*" (true)
Student D: "I ate horsemeat after going to a horse race. I felt sorry for the horse." (not true)

Question: "Students A, C, and D, was the horsemeat raw?"

Student A: "No, it was in a stew." (not true)
Student C: "Yes, it was." (true)
Student D: "No, it was a cooked steak." (not true)

*horsemeat 馬肉　terrible ひどい

9 Case Study: The Inheritance* ケーススタディ：遺産

30

A Japanese man and his wife are planning to go to Hawaii for their 50th anniversary*. They have two children, including one son, Yoji, who is divorced and has changed jobs several times, and one daughter, Yuri. Yoji has financial problems, and his parents loaned* him money that he has never repaid*. However, they haven't pushed him to repay them because they want to keep a good relationship with him.

Yoji told them that the trip to Hawaii is expensive and that they should save their money. However, the parents have enough money for the trip and suspect that he is concerned* that his parents are spending "his future inheritance." He has mentioned several times in the past that he is depending on* his inheritance to support his future and that he hopes to get a larger share of the inheritance, including his parents' house, since he is their eldest* child and only son. Yuri, the daughter, tells her parents to enjoy their life. She often visits her parents and tells them she will take care of them in the future. She is angry with Yoji and tells her parents to be more direct* with him.

*inheritance 遺産　anniversary 記念日　loan 貸す　repay 返済する
be concerned 心配する　depend on ~ ~による　eldest 一番年上の
direct 単刀直入な、はっきりした

Questions:

1. How should the parents handle future inheritance issues?
2. What is the best way for the parents to communicate about inheritance issues and other financial issues with their children?
3. Do you know a story about a family that had serious inheritance problems?
4. Do you think inheritance is "a right" or "a gift"?

Unit 11
Giving Opinions
意見を述べる

1 Activity: Fact or Opinion?
アクティビティ：事実、それとも意見？

A fact is a statement or information that is true and which you can prove. A factual statement: “Christmas is a popular American holiday.”

An opinion is a belief that may or may not be true (at least, not true for all people). An opinion: “Christmas is the most exciting holiday of the year in the U.S.”

Write “F” in the blank if the statement is a fact or an “O” if it is an opinion.
以下の 1 ～ 14 の空欄に、事実なら “F”、意見なら “O” を記入しましょう。

_____ 1. The first TV was made in 1928.
_____ 2. Dogs make the best pets.
_____ 3. About 70 percent of Americans are overweight and 30 percent are obese.
_____ 4. China has the largest population of any country.
_____ 5. All students should go to college for at least two years.
_____ 6. Kyoto was the capital of Japan during the Heian period.
_____ 7. Yukichi Fukuzawa founded Waseda University, and his face appears on ¥10,000 bills.
_____ 8. Abraham Lincoln was the greatest American President.
_____ 9. Americans eat more than two billion pounds of pasta per year.
_____ 10. The 2020 Summer Olympics was cancelled due to the coronavirus.
_____ 11. All people have their own unique fingerprints.
_____ 12. I'm too short.
_____ 13. Indian tigers are an endangered* species.
_____ 14. Pandas are the cutest animal.

*endangered species 絶滅危惧種

Now, find a reference to support two statements that you marked as a fact.
上記で「事実」“F” とした文の裏付けとなる文を書きましょう。

1. ____
____

2. ____
____

2 Case Study: Brown Sugar ケーススタディ：ブラウンシュガー

An American was hired to work in a famous, historical Japanese hotel known for excellent service. Patrick had graduated from Cornell University's hotel management program, recognized as the best hotel management program in the US. He was 23 years old. His first job placement at the hotel was to work in one of the hotel's restaurants. The manager of the restaurant was 63 years old, was a graduate of a vocational school (*senmon gakko*), and was scheduled to retire in two years.

The manager assigned Patrick to clean tables and to make sure such things as the salt and pepper shakers were full. At a staff meeting, the manager told the staff that he welcomed their ideas to improve the restaurant's service. Patrick was the first non-Japanese to be hired full-time by the hotel, so he thought it was a good opportunity to share his viewpoint* as a foreigner.

"The brown sugar we serve to customers who order oatmeal at our hotel is different from the brown sugar we use in America. I think we should offer a different kind of sugar," Patrick suggested.

The manager became angry. "You've worked here for six months. You don't know anything. You should keep your mouth shut unless I ask for your advice."

Patrick was often scolded by the manager. He had been called stupid, and once he was pulled into another room by his ear after he had made a mistake. The manager told Patrick that he wanted to have lunch with him to talk about his job performance.

Patrick was worried about this meeting, so he went to a Japanese friend, Shun, to ask for some advice about what to say during the lunch meeting.

*viewpoint 見方

Questions:

1. Why do you think Patrick experienced such a difficult time with the manager?
2. If you were Shun, what advice would you give Patrick?

3 Group Activity: The Values Shown by Japanese Words

グループアクティビティ：日本語に見る価値観

Look at the list of words and phrases below. In pairs or in a group, choose one of the words or phrases and then prepare to talk about it to the class, discussing the meaning of the word and the values the word reflects. During your presentation, imagine that you are talking to foreigners who know little about Japan.

枠内から単語やフレーズを選び、その意味や価値観についてグループの中で話し合い、クラスの前でプレゼンテーションをしましょう。聞き手は日本に関する知識が少ない外国人だと想定します。

Sonkei　Gaman　Senpai/kouhai　Sensei
Mottainai　Shudan koodoo　Kawaii culture
Honne/Tatemae　Menstu　Uchi/Soto
Giri　Yome/Shu tome

4 Activity: Presenting an Opinion アクティビティ：意見を述べる

32

The communication styles of Japanese and English speakers are often quite different, especially when giving opinions. When writing essays or giving a speech, for example, the Western approach to presenting an opinion is linear*, starting with an opening statement that presents the main point. All following points should then support the main point.

On the other hand, Japanese logic is traditionally more circular*. When Japanese express an opinion, they often start with background information and conclude* with the main point, though the Western approach is catching on.

Choose one of the following topics and then prepare to give a presentation. Use linear logic*: first, write an opening statement and then write the main supporting points. Three supporting points is enough, though you can choose to write more.

*linear 直線的な　circular 回りくどい　conclude 結論付ける　logic 論理

Young Japanese students should be given more time for play.
English should be taught from elementary school.
Men should do more child raising* and housework.
Japan should allow in more immigrants.*
Critical thinking should be taught in schools.
Governments need to do more to prevent* global warming.
The Japanese system of university entrance examinations* needs to change.
Women should take more company management positions.*

*child raising 子育て　immigrant 移民　prevent ~ ～を防ぐ
entrance examination 入学試験　management position 管理職

Opening statement: ______________________________

____

Supporting point #1: ______________________________

Supporting point #2: ______________________________

Supporting point #3: ______________________________

Supporting point #4: ______________________________

Supporting point #5: ______________________________

5 Activity: Mini-debates アクティビティ：ミニディベート

You will work in a debating team. Each member of the team will be given a different debate topic. Then you will have a turn to debate the topic with someone from another team. You will be given three or four minutes to prepare for your debate. Members of your team can give ideas, but only you should speak during the debate. During the rebuttal period, any team member may speak.

チームに分かれたら、先生がチームの代表にディベートのトピックを渡します。それぞれのチームメンバーはディベートのプレゼンテーションの準備に2分与えられます。チームメンバーはアイデアを提案できますが、話す人は1人です。反論の際は、どのメンバーも意見を述べることができます。

6 Activity: Debate アクティビティ：ディベート

How to Be an Effective* Debater

1. Do enough research to find strong support and then organize your points logically.
2. Speak clearly. Use simple language, speak slowly, and enunciate* well.
3. Remember some of your main speech so that you can speak smoothly* and have frequent* eye contact.
4. Use nonverbal communication* well, including eye contact, gestures, and a relaxed body posture. Also, use intonation and stress* for clarity* and feeling.
5. Be confident but not too strong or negative. Show respect and humility.*
6. Before the rebuttal, listen to your opponents' words and take notes.

*effective 効果的な　enunciate 明瞭に発音する　smoothly スムーズに
frequent 頻繁な　nonverbal communication 非言語コミュニケーション
stress 強勢・アクセント　clarity 明瞭さ　humility 謙虚さ

Debate Topics

- The government should force companies to promote more women to management positions.
- The retirement age should increase to 70 years old.
- Japan needs to change its constitution.
- Whale meat should be banned.
- Pet stores should be banned.
- Cram schools are still important.
- The internet should be censored.
- Any topic from page 83.

7 Case Study and Simulation: Pollution

ケーススタディとシミュレーション：公害

An American chemical factory is the largest employer* of people in a small town. Other people, such as shop owners, also depend on the factory, since many of their customers work in the factory. The factory, however, dumps* poisons* into the town's river, and the smoke from the factory makes the air dirty. Several children and older people have become sick from drinking the river water. Also, many residents* suffer from* asthma* and other breathing problems caused by the dirty air.

A meeting will be held to discuss this problem. Try to negotiate* a solution.

The people at the meeting include:

1. The town's mayor: This person wants to make the town clean so people can be healthier, but she/he doesn't want to hurt the factory, which is important for the town's economy. The town is pretty, but few visitors come because of the dirty air and water.

2. An environmentalist*: This person works for a national environmental group called CLEAN. She/he believes all companies must be responsible to clean up their pollution and make the environment safe. She/he often gets angry at "greedy* companies."

3. Company representatives*: They are concerned about the pollution, but the costs to clean the air (requiring* special technology, such as filters) and the river (requiring an expensive recycling system) are too high to pay all at once. If pushed too hard, they will move the factory to a town that is friendlier to them or, if that is not possible, just close the factory. These company executives live in a rich town about two miles up the river, away from the worst pollution.

4. Worker representatives: They are very worried about the health of their families, who live in the town. But they don't want the factory to close because they would lose their jobs and then have to move away.

5. A doctor: This person lives in the town and she/he will report on the medical problems caused by the pollution and give some recommendations about what should be done to make the environment safer for residents and their children.

6. (Optional) A government representative: This person works for the Environmental Protection Agency*. While the representative understands the economic problems the company and town face, she/he may threaten* to sue* the company if the river and air quality is not improved.

*employer 雇用者　dump 捨てる　poison 毒　resident 居住者　suffer from ~ ~に苦しむ
asthma 喘息　negotiate 交渉する　environmentalist 環境保護者　greedy 欲深い
representative 代表　require 必要とする　Environmental Protection Agency 環境保護団体
threaten 脅かす　sue 訴える

Unit 12

Self-Awareness

自己認識

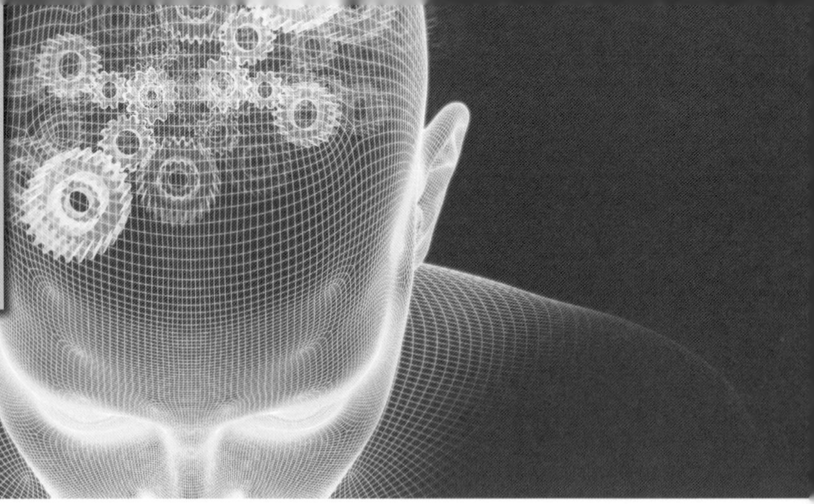

1 Reading: Self-Awareness

リーディング：自己認識

Knowing who you are and understanding how you see the world and how you approach various tasks and problems is important for effective critical thinking. However, it is difficult to really know yourself. To do that, we must be willing to look at our own thoughts, feelings, and motives*, including our own biases*. We must also be aware of how our history shaped us, including our cultures, our families, and our important life experiences. It is through a deeper understanding of ourselves that we can gain a wider world view, greater flexibility, and more powerful creativity and problem-solving skills.

Many people fear the process of getting to know themselves because they fear that they will not like what they see. Before starting your journey of self-awareness, it is important to know that no human is perfect. We all have problems, bad thoughts, biases, and even dark secrets. By trying to avoid them and hide them from others, we often build a wall around our growth and creative thinking. We become weaker because we are not real. Learning to be vulnerable* and to open our true selves to others helps us become stronger, more powerful, and better at critical thinking.

*motive 動機　　bias 偏見、先入観　　vulnerable 弱い、傷つきやすい

The benefits of self-awareness are:

1. It leads to self-growth and gives us the motivation to improve our lives.
2. It can make us better communicators and more effective problem solvers.
3. It helps us become more effective decision makers, including becoming better at avoiding problems and finding solutions.
4. It helps us become better listeners and better observers of others. With these skills, we can more easily understand the thinking and motives of others. This helps us improve all our relationships.
5. It makes us aware of what we need to do to become psychologically and physically healthier.

Read the following sentences. Write “T” if the sentence is true and “F” if the sentence is false.

以下の文章が内容と合っていれば “T”、合っていなければ “F” を空欄に書きましょう。

_____ 1. Most people already know themselves well without having to think so deeply.

_____ 2. We cannot know ourselves well without understanding how we became the way we are.

_____ 3. Knowing yourself can have a positive effect on your creative thinking.

_____ 4. If we share our problems and dark secrets, people will probably like us less.

_____ 5. Being vulnerable is risky and has few benefits.

_____ 6. Being self-aware helps us have better relationships.

_____ 7. Our physical and mental health are not really related to our self-awareness.

2 Activity: Imagine

アクティビティ：想像してみよう

Complete the sentences below. Any answer is OK, so feel free to use your imagination. After you have finished, share your answers in a group.

「もし自分が～だったら」という文を完成させ、グループ内でシェアしましょう。どんな答えでもオーケーです。想像力を駆使しましょう。

1. If I were a color, I would be ____________________.
2. If I were an animal, I would be ____________________.
3. If I were an object,* I would be ____________________.
4. If I were a kind of food or drink, I would be ____________________.
5. If I could choose any job, I would be ____________________.
6. What are some life events that made me who I am today?

   1. ____
   2. ____
   3. ____

*object モノ

3 Pair Work: How Healthy Are You?

ペアワーク：どのくらい健康ですか？

Read the following questions and circle your answers. Then ask the questions to your partner.

以下の質問に自分のこととして答えてみましょう。そのあとパートナーにも聞いてみましょう。

1. Which would you usually choose for breakfast?

A

B

C

D

2. Which would you usually choose for lunch?

A

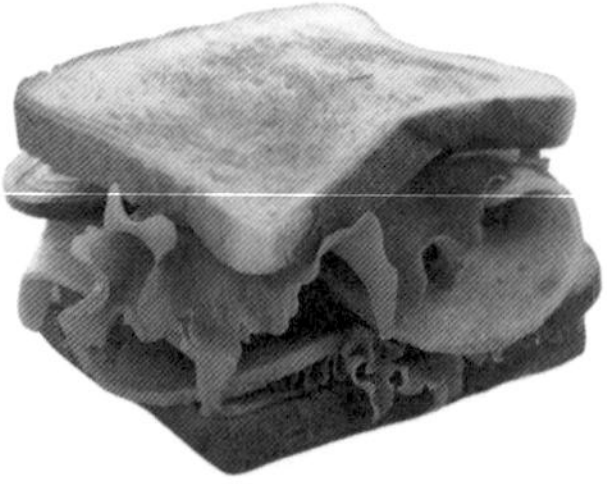

B

C

3. Which would you usually choose for dinner?

A

B

C

4. Which would you choose for a snack or dessert?

A

B

C

D

E

F

5. How many glasses of water or healthy drinks do you consume each day?

A Six or more glasses

B Around four glasses

C Three or fewer glasses

6. How often do you exercise each week?

A. Three times a week or more
B. Once or twice a week
C. Hardly ever
D. Never

7. How much sleep do you get each night on average?

A. Four to six hours
B. Six to seven hours
C. Around eight hours
D. Over eight hours

8. How often do you walk or bicycle each day?

A. Over* one hour
B. 30 minutes to one hour
C. Less than* 30 minutes

9. How often do you feel stressed?

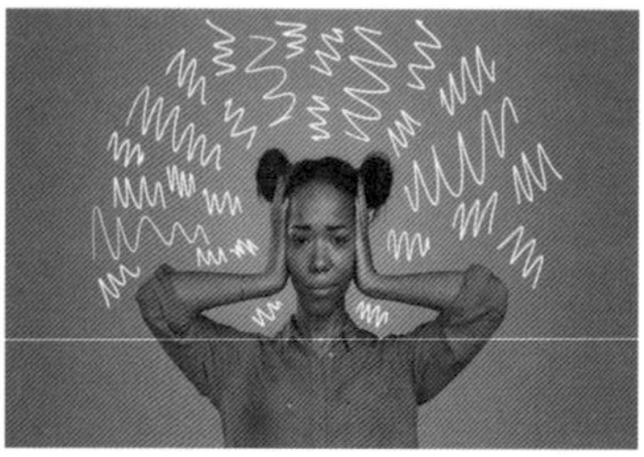

A. Very often
B. Often
C. Sometimes
D. Rarely*

*over ~　~以上　　less than ~　~以下　　rarely　めったに~ない

Writing: How can you improve your health?

1. ____________________
2. ____________________
3. ____________________
4. ____________________

4 Listening: Mindset リスニング：マインドセット

Dialogue 1

Tina: Are you studying for tomorrow's English test, Emi?
Emi: I don't like studying.
Tina: Do you want me to help you?
Emi: No. It's a waste of time*.
Tina: Why do you say that?
Emi: Because I'm not good at English.
Tina: But you did OK on your last test, didn't you?
Emi: Yeah, I guess so*. But that was just luck. I can't remember anything.
Tina: Really?
Emi: And I don't need to learn English anyway.
Tina: But English might be useful in the future for work or for traveling overseas.
Emi: Umm ... I don't think so. I don't even know what I want to do in the future.

*waste of time 時間の無駄 I guess so. たぶんそうだね。

Dialogue 2

Blake: What's your major, Ken?
Ken: Health and physical education*. I want to be a physical therapist* in the future.
Blake: Oh yeah?
Ken: Yeah, I'm really interested in helping people with physical problems.
Blake: How come?*
Ken: Well, I had a car accident when I was a kid and physical therapy really helped me. I'd like to help other people in the same way.

Blake: That's great! Is studying physical therapy difficult?
Ken: Yeah, at times, but I enjoy learning about the body and health. I want to be a good physical therapist in the future.

*health and physical education 保健医療学 physical therapist 理学療法士 how come? なぜ？

Questions:

1. Who do you think is more positive*, Emi or Ken? Why do you think so?
2. Who do you think is more negative? Why do you think so?
3. Which person might be more successful* in the future, Emi or Ken? Why?
4. Are you more often positive or negative?
5. Do you think it is possible* to change from being negative to positive? Why or why not?

*positive 前向きな successful 成功した possible 可能な

5 Reading: Mindset リーディング：マインドセット

37

Do you sometimes have thoughts like "I can't speak English," "I'm not good at math," or "I'm not good at sports"? These thoughts can hurt you. They can stop you from making progress* in life. This kind of negative thinking is called "a fixed mindset*." People who believe that they can learn new skills by trying their best* have "a growth mindset*."

Carol Dweck, a psychologist* at Stanford University, is famous for writing about "fixed mindset" and "growth mindset." People with a fixed mindset think they cannot change their intelligence or learn new skills. People with a growth mindset know they can learn new skills if they try hard. They can even become more intelligent*. Our minds are very powerful. Our thoughts can help us grow, or they can stop us from challenging new things.

If you have a fixed mindset, you are afraid of failure*. You want to look good all the time so that no one criticizes* you. Therefore, you avoid* new challenges or do not try hard. As a result*, you do not learn new skills. But if you have a growth mindset, you know failure is a part of learning new things. You do not give up easily. You learn from mistakes and criticism*.

Can a person with a fixed mindset change? Yes! Just take small steps. Challenge yourself to keep going when you fail or make mistakes. When you make progress, your confidence* will increase and you will try new challenges.

*make progress 進歩する　fixed mindset 硬直マインドセット　try one's best ベストを尽くす
growth mindset しなやかマインドセット　psychologist 心理学者　intelligent 知的
failure 失敗　criticize 批判する　avoid 避ける　as a result 結果として
criticism 批判　confidence 自信

True or False 内容把握

Write "T" if the sentence is true and "F" if the sentence is false.

以下の文章が内容と合っていれば "T"、合っていなければ "F" を空欄に書きましょう。

_____ 1. Having a fixed mindset helps us get new skills.

_____ 2. Carol Dweck believes intelligence cannot change.

_____ 3. People with a growth mindset like new challenges.

_____ 4. People with a fixed mindset are afraid of failure.

_____ 5. If you have a fixed mindset, you can change it to a growth mindset.

_____ 6. If you want to change, it is best to start taking big steps.

_____ 7. If you learn one skill, it can motivate* you to learn other skills.

*motivate やる気を起こさせる

6 Mindset Chart マインドセットチャート

How you feel about ...? こんなことに直面したとき どう感じますか？	**Growth Mindset** しなやかマインドセット	**Fixed Mindset** 硬直マインドセット
Challenges 困難	You want to keep learning. 学び続けたい You accept challenges. 挑戦をいとわない	You want to look smart. 自分は有能だと思われたい You avoid challenges. 挑戦することを避ける
Difficulties and mistakes 障害や失敗	You keep trying. トライし続ける You think about how to do better. どう改善できるか考える	You give up easily. すぐあきらめる You blame others. 人のせいにする
Criticism 批判・批評	You learn from criticism and mistakes. 失敗やミスから学ぶ	You get hurt and become angry. すぐに傷つき、怒りを覚える
Success of people around you 周りの人の成功	You are happy to learn from others' success. 他の人の成功から学びたいと思う	You feel bad and get jealous. 他の人の成功を脅威と感じ、嫉妬する

Now look at the various thoughts below, and then put the letters in the chart under Fixed Mindset or Growth Mindset. The first one has been done for you.

枠内には様々な“感情”のリストがあります。Fixed Mindset か Growth Mindset に分けてみましょう。

A. “I can never be good at math.”

B. “I can learn from my mistakes.”

C. “Losing weight is impossible for me.”

D. “She's better at making friends than me, so I will learn from her.”

E. “Oops, I made a mistake. Let me try again.”

F. “She's correct. I can do better.”

G. “I don't like criticism.”

H. “I'm naturally good at sports, so I don't need to practice.”

I. “I'm not good at English now, but I can study and get better.”

J. “I'm stupid*.”

* stupid　バカな

Fixed Mindset			Growth Mindset		
1. A	3. ____	5. ____	1. ____	3. ____	5. ____
2. ____	4. ____		2. ____	4. ____	

7 Running Dictation: The Story of Mina

ディクテーションゲーム：Mina の場合

You are now going to do a running dictation. Listen carefully to your teacher's instructions and have fun in this contest. Good luck!

ディクテーションゲームをしましょう。先生の説明をよく聞いてゲームを楽しみましょう。

8 Group Discussion: Hitting a Wall

グループディスカッション：壁にぶち当たったら

A

B

Questions:

1. What do these two pictures mean?
2. Which man has a fixed mindset and which has a growth mindset?
3. Do you have a fixed mindset about some things in your life? What are they?
4. Can you think of a "wall" in your life that you faced? Did you break through it successfully?
5. Who do you think is more likely to cheat, someone with a fixed mindset or someone with a growth mindset? Why?

9 Writing: Developing English Skills

ライティング：英語のスキルをみがく

Imagine you will move to England next year. What can you do to improve your English communication skills before your move? Write down several ideas below.

来年イギリスに引っ越すことになりました。その前に英語のコミュニケーションスキルを磨くにはどんなことをすればよいですか？　以下にアイデアを書きましょう。

1. ______________________________

2. ______________________________

3. ______________________________

4. ______________________________

5. ______________________________

6. ______________________________

What do you think about your English? Can you become good at English? Why or why not?

自分の英語力をどう思いますか？　英語力は上達すると思いますか？　なぜそう思うのですか？

10 Activity: Listening アクティビティ：リスニング

38

Listen to the story and fill in the missing words.

英語のストーリーを聞いて空欄を埋めましょう。

Today I'll tell you about a ______________________ ______________ who made many animation movies and cartoons*. His most famous character ________________ __________. Do ____________________? Of course, it's Walt Disney.

He ______________ in Chicago ______________. He loved __________ ________________________ and __________________________ when he ____________________. He started an animation company ________________ ____________________________, but it lost money and he had ______________ ______________.

He moved to Hollywood and ______________________________. He made a character called Oswald the Lucky Rabbit, which ________________________. But a business partner stole* the character and took away ____________________ ____________________________. Disney was shocked, but ________________ __________________.

In 1928, ________________ Mickey Mouse movie. It was very popular and ______________________________. He worked hard and ______________ ______________________ , such as "Snow White," "Cinderella," and "Bambi." __________________________ Disneyland, a theme park* near Los Angeles.

Walt Disney died* in 1966 when ______________________ ____________________. However, ____________________ ______________________ remember him and still __________ ____________________.

*cartoons アニメ（番組）、マンガ　　steal 盗む　　theme park テーマパーク
die 死ぬ

11 Presentation: Road to Success

プレゼンテーション：成功への道

Give a presentation about a person who faced difficult times but was finally successful. This person could be a family, or someone who is famous. Look at the story of Walt Disney in Activity 10 above as an example.

自分の周りの人たち、あるいは有名人で困難な課題に直面したにもかかわらず成功した人たちについてプレゼンテーションをしてみましょう。上の Activity 10 を参考にしてください。

Appendix 1 A

*top 勝る

Appendix 1 B

*nutrition 栄養　　bite ひとくち

Appendix 1 C

*ride 乗り物　　leave ~ breathless ～に息をのませる　　kiddy 子供　　amusement park 遊園地

Appendix 1 D

Don't let your first impression ...

... be the last thing people want.

Fresh Mints.
The first choice of people who don't always have fresh breath*.

*breath 息

Appendix 2

Memory Challenge 記憶力チャレンジ

1.

2.

3.

4.

5.

6.

7.

8.

9.

10.

11.

12.

13.

14.

Appendix 3

Example:

B: What's 8 down?

A: This is a verb. It's something you do when you want to make things neat.

B: Clean?

A: No. Let's say* you have a lot of books and you want to put them together by the type of book, such as textbooks, novels, comic books, and picture books. It's the opposite of "make a mess."

B: Organize!

A: Yes, that's it!

*Let us say 例えば

Student B

1		1 t			2 s	t	u	3 d	y		4 m	a	k	e	
		e			c										5 f
6		a			h			7	8 o		8 a	p	9 p	l	e
		c			o		10		r						e
		h			o				g			11 g			l
				12 p	l		n		13 a	f	t	e	r		
14 t	i	e		r					n			s			14
			15	o		15 m			i			t			
		16		b		i			z			u			
				l		16 s			e			r			
		17 s	18 e	e		t				19 a	g	e			
20			a	m		a		20 g		l					
			r			21 k		o		l			21		
22	22 h		n			e		d							
	a						23						23 m	a	p
	24 t						25 p	r	o	m	i	s	e		

Appendix 4

What does the following illustration show? Why is it important in intercultural communication?

以下のイラストをどう思いますか？　なぜこれが異文化間コミュニケーションに重要なのでしょう？

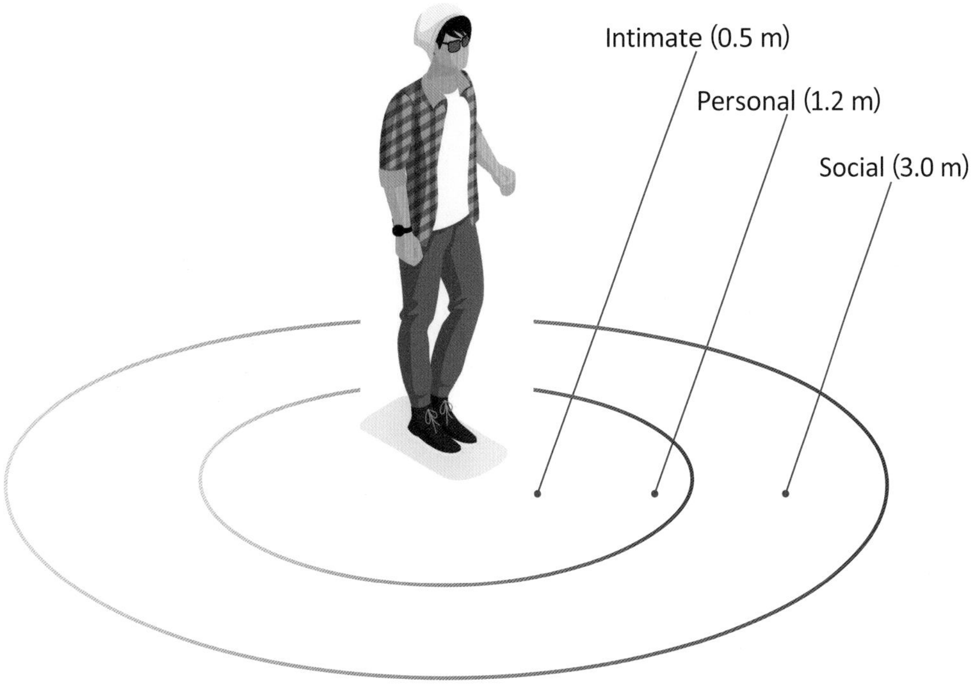

Appendix 5

A

B

C

D

E

Appendix 6A

Which world will you pass on to your children?

You can make a world of difference. Use sustainable* energy whenever you can. Just as important, contact your local politicians and demand greater use of sustainable energy. After all, it's your family's future.

The Council* for Sustainable Energy

CSENow@ html.com

*sustainable 持続可能な　　council 協議会

Appendix 6B

What are we really encouraging* women to become?

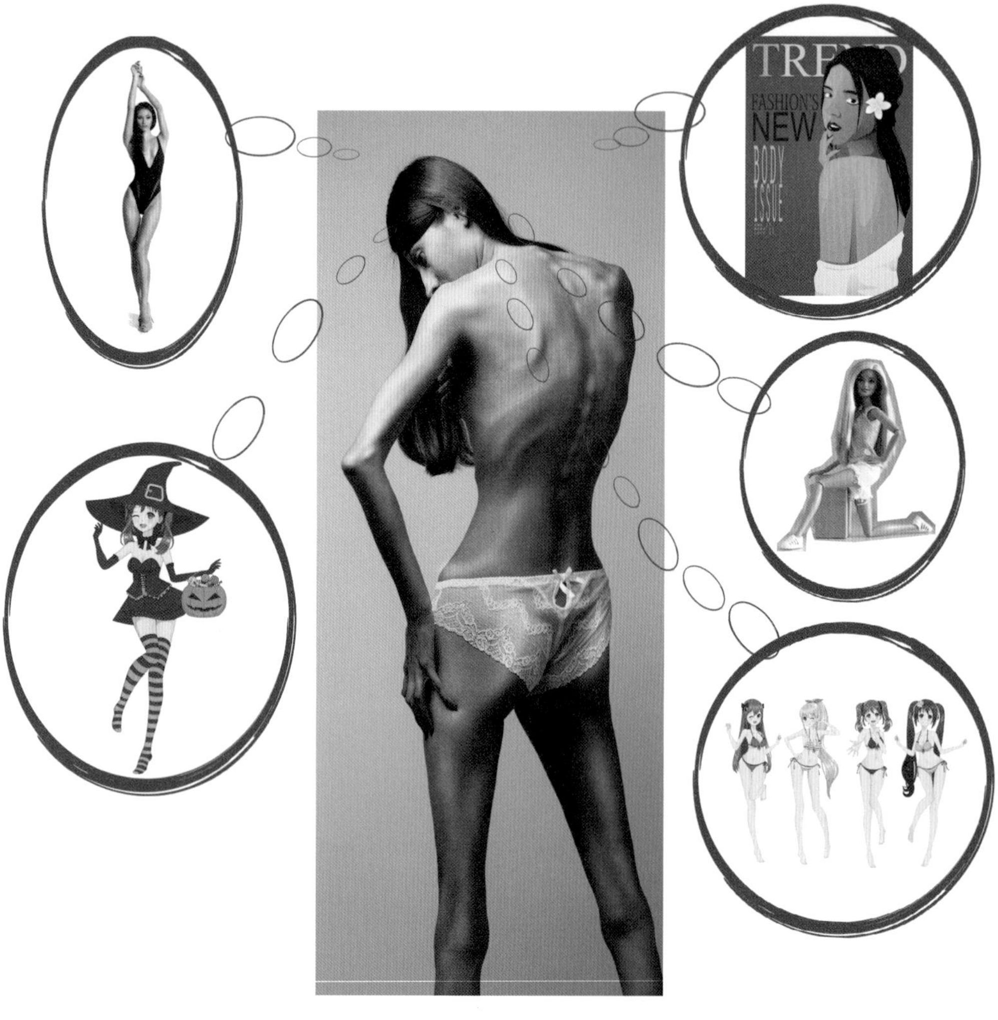

The images are all around us. The word "fat" haunts us. Don't buy into* it: Fear can make you (your daughter or female friend) skin and bones — or worse. Talk to your doctor, counselor, or contact us to get your mind — and body — in a healthy place.

Doctors to Prevent Anorexia
Contact us at Doc@rightthinking.com

*encourage 奨励する　　buy into 受け入れる

Appendix 6C

Some children get a bang out of* guns!

We have laws that ban children's books and children's toys. But why not guns??? Support legislation* for a gun-free life for our families.

The Committee for Gun-Free Living

*bang 銃をうつ音　　get a bang out of ~ ～をとても楽しむ　　legislation 法案

Appendix 7A

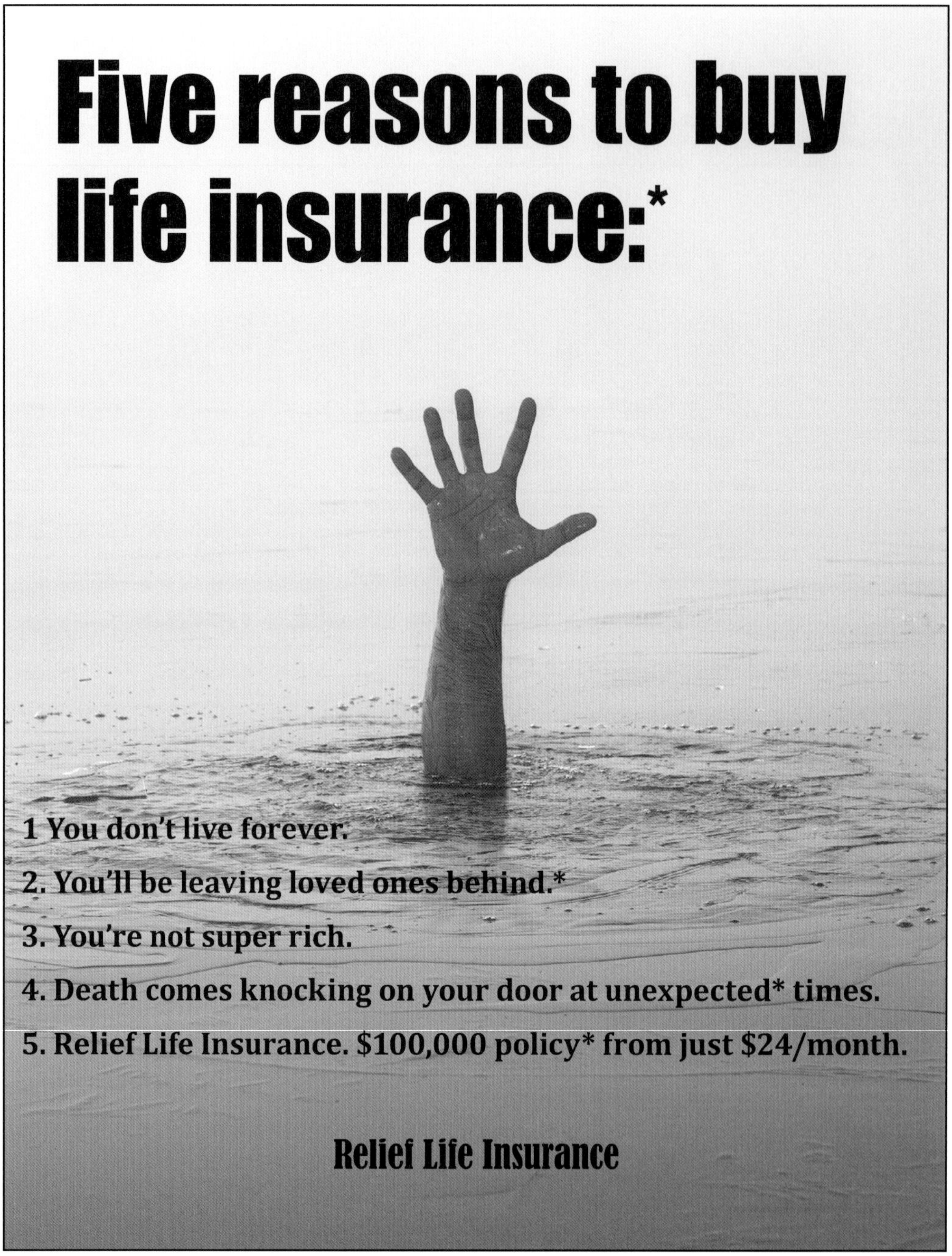

*life insurance 生命保険　leave 人 behind 人を置いてきぼりにする
unexpected 予想外の　policy 証書、証券

Appendix 7B

*wrinkle しわ　　buster 撲滅する人　　softener 柔らかくするもの

Appendix 7C

*diaper オムツ　　wee 小さな　　wee wee おしっこをする

Appendix 8

A

B

C

D

E

F

J

K

L

M

N

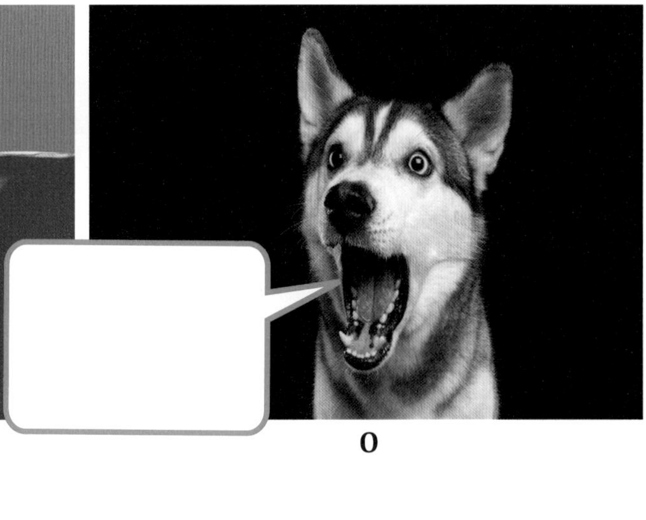

O

Speaking of Critical Thinking with Case Studies and Activities [B-919]
英語で学ぶ『クリティカル シンキング』

2 刷 2024年3月29日

著 者 Peter Vincent ピーター ビンセント
Naoko Nakazato 中里 菜穂子

発行者 南雲 一範 Kazunori Nagumo
発行所 株式会社 南雲堂
〒162-0801 東京都新宿区山吹町361
NAN'UN-DO Co., Ltd.
361 Yamabuki-cho, Shinjuku-ku, Tokyo 162-0801, Japan
振替口座 : 00160-0-46863
TEL: 03-3268-2311（営業部：学校関係）
03-3268-2384（営業部：書店関係）
03-3268-2387（編集部）
FAX: 03-3269-2486
編集者 加藤 敦

組 版 中西 史子

装 丁 銀 月 堂

イラスト さとう 有作 （p44, 47, 53, 54）

検 印 省 略

コード ISBN978-4-523-17919-1 C0082

Printed in Japan

E-mail : nanundo@post.email.ne.jp
URL : https://www.nanun-do.co.jp/